D0458424

North Bank

North Bank

CLAIMING A PLACE ON THE ROGUE

Robin B. Carey

Oregon State University Press
Corvallis

"Adam dwelt on the banks of the river, or in the land which was watered on eyther side, if we thinke good to take Paradise for that which is compassed about with rivers."

—John Calvin, *A Commentarie Upon Genesis*

The paper in this book meets the guidelines for permanence and durability of the Committee on Production Guidelines for Book Longevity of the Council on Library Resources and the minimum requirements of the American National Standard for Permanence of Paper for Printed Library Materials Z39.48-1984.

Library of Congress Cataloging-in-Publication Data
Carey, Robin.
North Bank : claiming a place on the Rogue / Robin Carey.
    p. cm.
ISBN 0-87071-448-1 (alk. paper)
1. Rogue River Valley (Klamath County-Curry County, Or.)—Description and travel. 2. Rogue River (Klamath County-Curry County, Or.)—Description and travel. 3. Rogue River Valley (Klamath County-Curry County, Or.)—Biography. 4. Carey, Robin. I. Title.
F882.R6C37 1998
979.5'21—dc21   98-25222
                                                                     CIP

Oregon State University Press
101 Waldo Hall
Corvallis OR 97331-6407
541-737-3166 •fax 541-737-3170
www.osu.orst.edu/dept/press

Contents

For Catharine—all the best years

Building with Bones

When my wife, Catharine, and I first aspired to be coastals, we lived in a rented cottage with its own short path down to the sand and the breakers of the Pacific. That was in a little community called Nesika Beach about midway between Gold Beach and Ophir, Oregon. But at the end of our first year there, the dresser drawers all swollen one inch out from flush and the clothes dank, we turned inland again and bought a place along the Rogue River. This new place wasn't far inland, only three miles from the coast by road, less than that on a straight line. But our move put the hump of Geisel Hill between ourselves and the Pacific.

The eastern slope of Geisel Hill felt calm and welcoming, out of the fog and the sea wind. It felt like inland places we had known before. Wind, at the right moments, howls very romantically, of course; but the wind at Nesika Beach had grown too commonly abusive for our sensibilities. It blew salt-slurry over our windows, and whipped rain into our faces at a near-horizontal slant. Looking at the new place as prospective buyers, we didn't think it mattered just how much cat hair had packed into the baseboard heaters of that cabin, how much water stain had spread across the fiberboard ceilings, or how much glaze had whitened the leaky thermalpanes, just so long as the place was out of the wind, someplace where we could regularly pull-to a door without a struggle.

There was, then, a sense of shelter to this Rogue cabin from the start, a home-quality. That was the idea—to make it home. This was in June. I watched red-tailed hawks circle in the thermals above the cabin. I felt at home with hawks.

I went out circling, as the hawks did, scouting out in arcs across the back hills to discover any paths we could use. It was rough going back there on the east slope of Geisel Hill behind the cabin, lots of slash. But the idea of home for me means knowing a place.

1

Learning the territory is a process I don't fully understand, but one that tugs at me with a feeling like necessity. Once beyond the stumbling beginnings of it, the process makes me feel nested and solidly on home ground. Anybody who cares about the land and who has gotten knocked from place to place in the transient society we call ours, knows about this process of re-creating the familiar, of remaking and reclaiming the landmarks. Because the North Bank is river country, the process out here starts with river pull-offs and river trails.

When the family lived in Wisconsin for a time, it was grouse hunting that led me out over the hills to the places that needed knowing, out to where the old farms tilted between hillsides, where the gray buildings sagged and fell, where the old harrows and wheels lay in the grasses, and the abandoned orchards put forth wormy apples for the grouse to feed on in the warm afternoons of Indian summer. In the upper Rogue Valley of other years, it was mountain quail that served the same purpose as those Wisconsin grouse.

But out here along the coast, the trees and brush grow too thick for much cross-country wanderings. Here the rivers were always the sites of settlement and travel. The old homesteads and schools stood near the rivers, the paths ran along the rivers, and what places I want to discover hold there, along the rivers, though I have not yet found so many of those places as to be dead certain just what they'll look like when I come upon them.

The inland cabin that we bought stands near this river world, on the north bank of a wide Rogue meander. The location could not be more convenient for my wanderings. From this point I can explore upstream toward Lobster Creek and beyond, or downstream toward the Wedderburn Bridge and the Rogue's mouth. South of us, and north of us, other coastal streams and creeks run their courses to the Pacific.

There will be different smells to these rivers than I have known elsewhere, different bird cries, and different beetles under different stones. There will be secrets at each bend, roadside secrets and trailside secrets. Gathering these will be my pastime. Learning these will be my study, as will the subtle ways that the strange turns known and then, at last, familiar.

Below our cabin, separating it from the Rogue, runs old U.S. Highway 101. New Highway 101, a straighter shot along the coast, renders this curve of old 101 mainly a local-access road. The locals call the old road simply "North Bank." The post office would have us add "Rogue" to distinguish this North Bank from North Bank Pistol, North Bank Chetco, North Bank Winchuck, North Bank Smith. I glimpsed the full name once on a rusted signpost: "North Bank Rogue River Road." Most of the local rivers have north bank roads, popular residential roads, too, because the sun in a south sky slants down to them and warms them. The sun ripens up the tomatoes in the sag-fenced garden patches and discourages moss on the rooftops. The south bank, for its part, mostly languishes in shadow.

From our cabin we couldn't see the Rogue at first. Myrtlewoods and pines screened the front of the place. We could see the air corridor above the river, though, that corridor where the gulls and the terns flew. Kingfishers dipped and chattered there. Mergansers wheeled in flocks upstream. An occasional eagle floated high in the thermals. After a rain, swallows glided delicately back and forth above the river. At dawn, sometimes, the clouds hanging low over the river corridor rose almost vertically with some thermal upthrust of river air. Then, too, we could hear the Mail Boats go by, and could hear the drone of the Mail Boat drivers' voices intoning information. They all stop their boats somewhere out front of the place and spout for awhile. Something monumental around here inspires these speeches, but I don't know what, unless it's the way the main river channel has moved clear over to the south leaving only a residual back-channel here on the north side, known locally as "The Snag Patch."

Four acres of fir stand on the back slope behind our cabin, a few more down in the seasonal-creek draw, mixed with some enormous tan oaks, rotted on the uphill side ("cat-faced" the locals say), and a maze of myrtlewoods, pines, and holly in the front. Despite the corridor of river birds, the uprising clouds, and the summer sounds of Mail Boats, we hardly realized at first how close the Rogue River ran by us. Not until I asked our new neighbor, Neighbor S., if I could cross his land, not until I had crossed the North Bank Road, cut a swath through Neighbor S.'s blackberries, walked a plank across Edson Creek, waded the Snag Patch channel, and crossed a stretch of willow-thicket island, did I find that stretch of river called Johns Riffle, named for a fisherman, Jacob Johns. I turned there to look north and west, and saw then how the bend of river above me ran not so very far at all from the tall firs of our side border.

Various local chain saw specialists advertise in the *Curry County Reporter* their skills at dropping trees and cutting "windows" through blocking foliage, accommodating the viewing passion. The faller who showed up at our door for an estimate had sly-looking eyes, bulky shoulders, a pointed nose, a thin brown beard. It happened we knew in common a teacher, this timber faller one of her former students. As he told me stories of how she had thrown chalk and erasers at various uncooperative students, of how she had once pulled her hair in a rage of frustrated pedagogy, he took evident pleasure in bouncing his shoulders up and around in their sockets, and hooking his thumbs under his suspenders.

"Yup. Old Sara. I surely do remember her."

His partner, the topper, when he came, laced his climbing-pacs with a deft weaving of one hand, and carved a small glimpse of river for us, out to the south, between the limbed trunks of two girthy firs, a glimpse sufficient for me to peer past a post on the front stoop and see "the view."

It is not "the view" that particularly interests me, however, but rather just where the winter water level runs. The naked eye manages that task in pleasant weather, but when rain or fog is blowing, binoculars help. What I see through those dusty optics, additional to the river itself and the occasional winging mallard or merganser, is a slanting gravel road on the far south bank, and below it a straggly line of brush cross-woven with high water flotsam, mostly dead leaves wrapped and pressed to those brush stalks like rags to a yard pipe. This brush line is my marker, my point of reference. If the river runs below brush line, then I can wade the Snag Patch channel, and Johns Riffle is low enough, and clear enough, for a fly.

Our cabin sits perhaps one hundred feet above the river, the angle of view too oblique to make out the river's color. Generally the river-glint turns even muddy water to silver. It's mostly true that low water translates to clear water, but not always. The other day, having finished some new casements and brushed on the first coat of varnish, I pulled into my waders, laced my wading boots, grabbed my fly rod, and headed down the driveway. Three red-tails screamed at me from above. I wondered if the odd one out was an interloper or a hang-about juvenile. Down at the road, I put an outgoing letter in the mailbox, cut down through the blackberries, crossed Edson Creek, pushed through some myrtlewood, slid down a clay bank, and slogged across the Snag Patch. The usual flock of ducks— mallards this time—got up below me as I reached Johns. Watching them, I took four steps into the river before seeing that the water ran thick brown. Some fellow up by Galice, I learned later, someone deaf to regulation, had drained a mining pond into the Wild and Scenic Rogue.

Nonetheless, the view helps gauge the river, and gauges more than the Rogue. At midbrush level the smaller coastal streams will be running green through their canyons. Some fall mornings, however, I gauge fishing sentiment without the view at all, and easily, for a heavy droning at dawn of fishing boats headed up from the Port is always a sign of promise.

My father would have loved this place, would have sat in the summer sun on the stoop, Johns Riffle glinting over his right shoulder, the violet-green swallows darting in and out of their nesting hole under the eaves, the blue herons flapping low over the house from their Snag Patch fishing to their rookery in Neighbor H.'s back pines, uttering somber rasps and rattles to their young. That sound fills the summer air here as constantly as the winter's is filled with a gushing of seasonal creeks. And the strung-along jibber my father uttered after his stroke, his raspy oddities, almost as baffling and strange as the speech of herons, maybe said this to me: "I've saved a little money. Take it, when I die, and buy some place where you can see a river."

I suppose, in the certain ways I live, the certain habits I lean to, my father has his presence, and I don't begrudge it, particularly that tendency of mine to fish seriously. Then, too, there are those foxed and faded first editions of his scattered around our bookshelves, and his old tackle box in the garage full of tooth-raked wooden plugs. Those leavings add their qualities to the character of this place.

When I think of my father, I remember those stormy days he favored for his fishing. He knew how walleyes fed when heavy waves churned up the shallows. The winds of those fishing days blew up some intimidating waves under us on some big Minnesota lakes, but those winds never lasted too long. Get winds of that kind in youth, and they seem like the right winds. They blow, and then they stop, and they make the incessant Nesika Beach winds seem wrong. On the North Bank we sometimes get a howling, tree-bending wind that pounds pinecones into our windows. But after a few hours it stops. It feels right, and sets me to remembering Minnesota thunder and that yellow, tornado-coming storm-light of certain summer afternoons.

The wraith of my father, puffing his pipe on the North Bank stoop, knows all about these winds, and about fishing compulsions, that excitement in the belly. He'll probably not stay on the stoop for long, but drag himself down to the river, crawl or roll if necessary, land a fish at all costs, and keep his pipe lighted through the whole process. The ghost image of him, there on the stoop, gives this North Bank cabin a familiar and homey quality, something like the feeling cast by those clan portraits hanging on the interior walls.

It is late February now. We've seen some good rains. The Edson Creek Frog Chorus has begun a nightly rehearsal, a single monotonic fluting that sometimes quiets on an instant, some coon hushing them down with its hunt. Herons are flying steadily back and forth from the Snag Patch to the back pines. I can't see what they're doing back there, but it must be nest improvements occupying them, home building.

They're working on their floors, probably, maybe their edgings, and building with flotsam. I'm working on the long-neglected cabin walls, building with memories of how a cabin should look, memories of northern Minnesota cabins, and of Wisconsin sand-country cabins. And the ambiance of this place feels right. When the big North Bank myrtlewoods wave in the yard, and across the road, they remind me of those midwestern cottonwoods I watched from my bedroom window as a boy. One myrtlewood, down on the northeast corner of the lot, is so large in the bole that I could put a chair up there between the first branchings. The coons know the place; it is always filled with their sign and with a faint odor of coon. These are different trees from the cottonwoods, of course, these myrtlewoods, evergreen, and with their own perfumed smell, but their tops blow properly in winds, and the distant emotions they generate in me make this North Bank place feel true and right, what the Swedes and Norwegians must have felt when they found Minnesota, what my distant Hollander kin must have felt when they found Lake Michigan and remembered the North Sea. Such memories, dim though they are, yet take hold of my hands with the plane and the saw, guide the hammer strokes against the boards, and I build with this flotsam, these memories, these bones.

Steelhead runs are spotty. Yesterday on a slick I ran into a giant fellow with a full brown beard and a front tooth missing. He carried a shoulder bag and a spinning rod, some pencil-weight dangling from the arced tip of the rod. "Nothing gives," he said. "But they should be in there. They should be in there." A kind of bewilderment showed in his repetition. He shrugged and wandered on past me. "I'll just try it down here," he said over his shoulder.

I'd fished all morning, myself, over some pretty good drifts, a two-inch rain just clearing away. One half-pounder was all I'd touched, wild and jumpy, but not one of those freight train chromers of February. The rancher who'd let me fish his place drove up. His black Stetson knocked the pickup roof when he turned to ask how I'd done, and his look turned perplexed when I told him. He pushed back his hat. "Should be good now with that rain," he said. "Wonder how the professionals are doing, Milt and Earl."

That rancher had about twenty sheep climbing the back end of his pickup, trying to get at the hay bales. "Well, I better get to work," he said, checked the rearview mirror, and backed his truck around. He nudged a couple ewes out of the way with his fender, dropped down off the road into the grassy field toward the white humped ribs of a winterkill, and let me pass by.

It's an empty, wistful wonderment inside that goes with the phrase, "They ought be in there." But a couple months ago I drove up to Cape Sebastian with my binoculars and watched gray whales spouting all along the sea's horizon. They're in there now in a way they haven't been for years, come back from endangerment to abundance. And the next day an Oregon Department of Fish & Wildlife (ODFW) staffer, Dave Harris, told me, all smiles, "There's a great run of steelhead coming into the Chetco, big and bright. We got some in our nets." Another ODFW man, the local director, Tim Unterwegner, told me of the Rogue this winter, "We're doing about as well as anybody in the state."

Last winter I got a call from a commercial fisherman I know, John Wilson, who asked if I'd help him with some hatch boxes up on Coy Creek, a creek not far at all from the North Bank place.

John and I beat through blackberries all one morning unearthing old PVC piping, fixing the breaks. By noon we had water, cold and beautiful. I'd worn work gloves. John hadn't, and wore a couple dozen stickers in his sea-weathered, salt-cured hands. When John trucked down ten thousand eyed chinook eggs from Elk River

Hatchery, and the water started perking through them in their hatch boxes on the platform above Coy Creek, we both felt pretty good. We stood there on the freshly swept platform, newly cleaned and rocked hatch boxes at our feet, fresh water gurgling in the scrubbed-out storage tank, purple eggs rocking in a gentle wash, and felt a fatherly expansiveness run through our veins.

Coy Creek is a feeder stream of Euchre Creek, and wild-stock salmon have been all but extinct in Euchre Creek for some years now. A decade back the watershed streambeds got used as skid roads in logging operations, and the banks scalped to the stream edges. Step out into Euchre Creek today, years after the logging, and you sink down a foot at each step. The creek is still cleaning itself of the accumulated silt of that period, washing it a few more yards downstream with each winter flooding.

Not so many years ago there were salmon in Euchre Creek so thick that up at that old cabin above the forks they'd kick one out for the dogs to eat whenever one was needed. Sometimes they'd cook it and sometimes they wouldn't, just toss it into the dog run. The going was easy along the creek back then, too, because the timber was big and the bears made fishing paths, wide and well trampled. These things I learned yesterday from Neighbor S., seventy-six years old, not looking it, I told him, honestly. "But I goddamn feel it," he said.

Last week I hiked a cross-country slant from a high contouring logging road down into the roadless upstream canyon of Euchre Creek, followed thorny seeps and elk trails, and hit the stream several miles up from the last road. Three brown humps moved in the water, otter backs. I watched them through the thick new-growth alder until they porpoised around the bend. Then I stepped out into the water. The gravel was firm and crunchy. The pool below was deep and clean. Two small fish held in the current, smolts I thought. I crisscrossed the bends back to the road, climbed over and under blow downs, and saw new-scoured pools. The old wounds are healing.

It's not always a blessing to have known the earlier days the way Neighbor S. knew them, not an easily evident blessing anyway. Memories of plenty carry with them a pressing nostalgia. My own West Coast nostalgias need looking at some because they shape the paradigms of plenty that I live with and build upon, a plenty diminished a little from Neighbor S.'s early days, but still a plenty. Those memories began on the Quinalt River of the Olympic Peninsula. I waded out into it, that first morning, with leaky hip boots and a couple of spinners. Before I'd worked down past the first bend, I'd hooked one enormous salmon, two steelhead, and a sea-run cutthroat. I decided maybe the West would be a place I'd like to stay, to make home.

A long-muscled old man in a neighboring campsite told us we should have some high-bush cranberries to go with the one steelhead I'd kept, and showed us where to find them. He was right about the mix.

"One other thing," he said as he left the next morning. "Always hunt your elk uphill from your rig. Remember that." And he drove away with an unspoken certainty on his face that I would stay in those parts and need his advice. He was right about that, too. We settled in Oregon.

Ashland, Oregon, was a sleepy little town when we moved there, not yet the destination theater town of present times. I found a couple of fishing friends at the state college. We'd drive up to the upper portion of the Rogue River any afternoon we could get free, and wade out at Casey Park, or upstream from there at McCloud Bridge.

The first time we drove up to fish the upper Rogue, its famous name buzzed in my head as I rode along, two of us new to the place, tenderfeet, riding in back, two river veterans riding in front, talking the language. At the river, then, the veterans went their ways, wading off through spawning salmon in the shallows. We two new fellows, slow at gear-rigging, finally waded out to cast. Dave, below me, cranked partway into another long sentence about Ohio, then went half-cocked silent. I looked downstream in time to see his rod tip slide beneath the surface and a torrent of bubbles rising.

The Rogue is a deep and ledgy river. It can get skittish with unwary immigrants.

We'd park at the McCloud Bridge, myself growing gradually familiar with that stretch of the Rogue, and walk down through the dry grass to the top of a half-moon drift, about a hundred yards of riffle filled with planted rainbow and the occasional Rogue summer-run steelhead. Almost always some slack and hook-jawed salmon carcass lay wrapped on a log, another drying on the beach, emitting elemental perfumes. I'd cast a saggy line and a knotty leader, hook a steelhead, and lose the fish with a snap. It happened over and over that summer, my casts not worth putty, my blood-knots worse. Sometimes there was a skinny-dipper or two around the bend, a man with bony white shoulders and flaring black beard, a woman with hair down to her bare bum. "Don't bother us if it don't bother you," he'd say, and I'd fish on by them, extra careful with my backcasts.

Those are my nostalgias—days of plenty, days of high-bush cranberries, days of learning my knots. These days on the North Bank I sit at the oak table under the kitchen swag-lamp, the Edson Creek frogs droning, a territorial cat-hiss now and again sounding behind the cabin, and I tie elegant leaders with good, solid blood-knots. Deer chew under the apple trees, tame as cattle, eyes gleaming out of the darkness, and the rolling loop of running line in my hands turns perfectly over the shooting head, pulls tight, and holds. Nylon circles between my thumb and finger, circles again, pulls through, and the perfection loop draws tight exactly to its name. I use micrometer and measuring tape, consult my log of experiments, and run elementary calculations of weights and diameters. Last month I devised a flyline by splicing a high-density tip to an old braided belly, then the belly to a new plastic-coated running line. Tying the splices, I peeled off coating down to the nylon core, divided strands with a needle, stroked and twisted the fuzz of each end to three prongs, waxed and interlaced those, twisted them tight, wrapped them smooth with a gyrated bobbin, then coated them with a mixture of Goop and Meek. The splices slide through my rod guides like eels, hardly a touch of resistance.

The whole process reminds me a little of the way I've put together my life in different sections of the country, of the way most of us have put together our lives, smoothing together the transitions, testing the splices. There's a backing line out of Minnesota, a running line out of Seattle, a belly-section out of Ashland, and now these delicate gradations of North Bank tippet. With my micrometer I could measure the years.

An old fellow up at Lobster Creek the other day nudged his Labrador out of the way with one muddy boot and allowed as how he'd done some fly-fishing. He'd seen me returning from fishing on the south-bank riffle and come out of his camper to chat, the Lab prancing around with a raised ruff and uncertain bark.

"Oh Christ yes," he said. "Christ, absolutely. Hardly a California river I haven't fished with a fly. Always could do better with a fly than anything else. Tied my own, too."

He said this last as though it were the true touchstone of the fishing breed, looked over the Street Walker variant on my line, just eyed it without my intending to show it to him in any particular way, and said, "Hummmmm."

I was wet from a hard winter wade, and remembering the perfect form of an egret that had sailed off the far-side gravel bar ahead of me.

The old fellow talked about the Klamath, how he'd fished that river years back for steelhead, down low somewhere, what was the name of that town?

"Weitchpec? Orleans?" I said, unlacing my boots, remembering Weitchpec, and Orleans, and the Yurok toughs, and the old road down to Pecwan.

"No," he said. Then, "Orleans. Orleans. That's it."

"Nice canyon below town, down to Bluff Creek."

"Absolutely," he said, brightening. "Caught a lot of fish down there. Used to tie up a Silver Hilton, good little fly on the Klamath."

It was a good fly on the Rogue as well. I'd tied them, fished them, lost them at McCloud, at Casey, heavy hooks on thin leader, a foolish combination, and said so.

The old fellow and I stood there remembering in the cold river wind, reworking landscapes, shaping our Rogue scene with Klamath parts, the Labrador sniffing at my leg, maybe scenting the dig-it-up method. I scratched the dog's ears, and wondered, as I had wondered some times before, just who was remembering what, reinventing what, in naming a bark-sided boondocks Klamath River place like that Orleans.

Could be some displaced kin of mine, I suppose, hammering with dreams, building with bones, taking some cross-the-sea remembered place upcurrent past the sea winds of Requa, past Kenek and Weitchpec, to that wide, sand-spitted, inland bar at the river curve. Whoever it was, I'd guess, sat down to lunch somewhere along that tangled Klamath riverbank, imagined himself back on a remembered curve of the Loire, and called the place Orleans. And he did so, I think, simply because of some familiar scent in the air, or because a prompting turn of sky blew into view, or because a bird sat a branch just so in silhouette, or because of any of a hundred-odd other possibie reasons for memory, from the cut of his bread to the lace of his shoe.

I was learning at the North Bank place just how that all worked, that home-claiming process, how the memories of family and landscape and former homesteads prompted recollection. The more I thought about the matter, the more I understood that French fellow, whoever he was, down there on the Klamath River, and how he came to name that wild river bar Orleans.

~

Home River

In the study of the North Bank cabin hang two black-and-white photographs. One shows our long-deceased Labrador, Nipper, lying beside propped shotgun and boots, light glinting off the tip of her nose, in the doorway of a deserted cabin. The other, titled "Christmas Day, 1979," shows a similar old cabin, weathered, bleached, and sagging, my daughter looking out one paneless window frame of it, one hand up over her eyes to shade them, my son looking out the other window frame, a dark, empty doorway between them, and snow on the hills of Grizzly Mountain, behind. Both of these pictured places lie over in Bear Creek Valley, a drainage of the upper Rogue.

Abandoned cabins and fallen farmhouses are the stuff of photographic cliché, of course; but that fact doesn't much matter to me. Art is not the point of these photos. The point is to remember those places and how I once knew them, how I hiked out to them, wallowed around in their nostalgia, moved some mental furniture through the sagging door frames, and restructured the past. The point is to remember those yellowed newspapers on the walls, and how I dug around through the mouse turds and broken glass, kicked over some boards, and watched the sow bugs scatter. At those fallen homesteads there's a nice open view across the front hillsides, and an outhouse in back as bleached as the bones of a winterkill. The photographs hanging in the North Bank cabin remind me of those Bear Creek inland valleys and those cabins I once found there.

The pair of boots in the picture with Nipper was an extra pair I packed out to the one cabin and tossed on the stoop. That's tampering with reality, of course, not tried-and-true documentary style. I told Nipper to lie down in the doorway, leaned my Model 12 Winchester against the door frame, and set up the camera tripod. After some meter readings of light and some figuring of the zones, I shot brackets. Now, when I look at this picture, finished and framed,

I feel like I'm inside that cabin on the bedsprings taking a snooze after a hard morning of chasing pheasants. It's a pleasure to lie there as inert as a fallen timber and to have off those heavy boots. Nipper stands guard in the doorway to scare off wandering porcupines or any of those brazen flickers that favor the place. Breezes blow across my chest and feet and tug at the ghost curtains. This place is mine, I've arranged it, I own it, it's been willed to me by an imagined grandfather, his moustache drooping down to his chin. He crossed the plains in a Conestoga wagon and probably found some gold up the rocky back draw to the east.

In the truth of things, though, one grandfather never got further west than Oklahoma Territory, and jumped around down there so much, from town to town, that even the relatives called him "fiddlefooted." The other grandfather, the one I favor, never got west either, but raised a family on Mississippi river bottom, farmed the richness of it, and found his forty acres of Illinois a steady and sustaining place. When Catharine and I took the kids for outings on Grizzly Mountain, old-cabin country, one valley or another, we found those valleys and their cabins steady and sustaining places, too, in their own ways. We could even call those places ours since a lot of that land, the higher part, falls in public domain, that rocky hilltop land that nobody much ever wanted and that defaulted to BLM scrub. Certainly the badgers and the bobcats didn't appear to worry much about survey stakes on those hillsides, and in our imagining we could take what we wanted of that land any day of the week.

Knowing exactly where the home place abides takes some mental adjustments sometimes, because home can be someplace to leave, or someplace you can't go back to because it's gone, or it's changed, or you've changed. I got melancholy for half an hour or so one night in front of the old family house in Milwaukee, before I realized it was the wrong house, remodeled to look more like the right house than the right house itself. An ash tree added the final confusion. The ash I remembered in our front yard was no longer there, and the neighbor's ash had grown up to about the right dimensions. The wrong house looked right; the right house wasn't home anymore. It was a shell game, and all that shell game of memory only goes to make true home-feelings the more valuable where I find them, even on BLM scrub.

The home river is an easier concept, or I choose to make it easier. Under the river's surface, as Bernoulli explained, flows a laminar slowdown of some complexity. But you don't need to go that deep. With rivers you can bounce your gaze off the surface, like light, and the reflection feels natural and sufficient. One of the Psalms says that the river of God is filled with water. So is the home river filled with water. The gaze might wander, the light might fade, but the water is there.

Not too far north of Ashland ran the North Umpqua River. Its summer-run steelhead arrived sporadically in late June, then more heavily in July and on through November. They stacked up in a thirty mile stretch of river designated fly-fishing only. The stretch held then, and still holds, balmy fishing most summer days, up until the first freezing mornings of October. The North Umpqua was the first river I claimed in any enduring way, set the heart's flag in midstream and rocked it solid.

I took myself pretty seriously as a fly-fisher on the North Umpqua, struck a few classic poses for the roadside tourists with their binoculars, tried to fish the far side of the river more than necessary, in love with the long cast. The mirror of the river always flowed at my feet. I tend to remember the North Umpqua that way—posed and formal.

But North Umpqua times were good times. There was an honesty and clarity to the Umpqua and its codes. Frank Moore's Steamboat Inn, even when the "Yes, We're Closed" sign was in the window, always had the back door open. People came in, made coffee, picked up some flies, or a flyline, or a pair of waders, and wrote down what they took, or left money under the counter. They told the truth about what they took, and, mostly, about what they caught.

This was pretty much catch-and-release fly-fishing. Unlike meat-fishing, which jumps firmly on a certain logic, catch-and-release fishing, like religion, works out into realms of faith. To the North Umpqua came fly-fishers of many sorts, greater and lesser sorts, subordinate to the river. They spoke quietly. They got up early. They stood in the river like pilgrims in the Ganges. When the sun reached the water, and the mist lifted, they moved to a shady bend or canyon for midmorning fishing, or went back to the Inn, or to some campground, and had coffee.

The river's codes, like Roman law, had a certain civilizing influence. Most fly-fishers learned a kind of parental regard for the steelhead runs, and a lot of fly-fishers, myself included, put in some time planting trees along the tributaries, or building gabions to collect spawning gravel, and in the process got themselves personally invested in steelhead survival. Proprietary feelings are home feelings, I realize. I'll need to do some investing like that along the North Bank of the Rogue if this splicing of allegiances is going to work.

My initial fishing skills never posed much challenge to the North Umpqua runs. I put in a year thrashing the river with a four-piece pack rod and catching nothing. My first Umpqua hook-up happened one day when Frank Moore saw me along the road, pulled over in his pickup, his wire-haired mutt Mokey whining in back. Frank looked me over, evidently decided I had done enough hard-time in the trenches of ignorance, and said, "Climb down over there. Stay low. Wade in *behind* that boulder, not *on* it. Cast just past the tip of that next boulder."

He drove away, and the steelhead he had steered me to took my fly with a startling enthusiasm. She ran deep into the reel's backing before she jumped, and I saw the distant airborne streak of her below the Fall Creek rapids. Rumor had it that each season Frank jogged up and down the riverbanks climbing trees, peering down into the pools, charting the steelhead lies of the river. Part of it all was knowing where they lay.

My regular fishing partner took a summer job at Steamboat Inn, got trained in as a part-time guide, passed his information on to me, this in exchange for some bird hunting savvy. We'd drive along the river, and Mike would be pointing here and there.

"Frank says they hold over there against that far bank. It's a long cast."

"That's a place Frank fishes in winter. It's no good in low water."

"Frank says you can catch them here right up in that white water, way up high."

The talk went on like that, along mile after mile of river. Thirty miles holds a lot of chutes and lies to remember. There still are strange places on the North Umpqua for me, and other places that take some hard remembering. Most of them, too, you can only learn by fishing; they fish different than they look. Being shown a few places at the beginning teaches what to look for, gives a feel for that steady, silky, bubbly drift of current that steelhead favor. But I never much liked being guided, and all those tips about just where to fish, and how to fish there, I tended to forget.

Certainly the North Umpqua gave me perspective on my fishing compulsion. Mine was no great compulsion at all, comparatively speaking. I never slept all night on the island rocks of The Station, just to be the first one on it come morning, and never raced anyone down the road to Wright Creek where the hatchery fish stacked up. I was only one of those who headed out before dawn, one of those ghostly cruising drivers out in the moonless fog, thinking maybe to be the first one to Upper Archie, or to The Ledges, or to Fairview. I was seldom the earliest of this breed, either, and another fly-fisher would be at my chosen spot before me, car parked dark in the pull-off, maybe a cigarette glowing behind the windshield. And code was code, fair was fair, first was always first. I'd head on down to the next lie on my mental list—Split Rock or Coleman or Rattlesnake. Others did the same for me.

On the North Umpqua it was easy to find the pull-offs, the well-beaten paths down through the timber. Most North Umpqua fly-fishers wore cleats of some kind, too, and you could tell the favored casting places by the scratches on the rocks. Sometimes you could even trace your way out a tricky wade to some ledge or island by following scratch-paths on the underwater boulders. Probably because these places were so open to discovery, the better fly-fishers favored hard-casting, hard-wading lies where the river disposed of apprentices. I always liked those places where someone had cut a swath of brush behind to make room for backcasting. I figured the cutting work meant fish out front somewhere, always a comforting nostrum.

Or there were ways to fish the easy lies that caught the hard fish—like Fairview, a long white ledge along the shore, two easy lies high up, one easy lie low down, and a last place way across and down that few fly-fishers touched. Of course, so that the fish didn't spot you on the riverbank and spook, you first had to follow the path through the culvert under the road.

September was my favorite month on the North Umpqua, and late September the time of a ritual last trip before fall-term teaching began. Mike Baughman, Jim Dean, and I would head up to the river, camp at Bogus Creek, or Island, sometimes at Canton Creek, sometimes at the old Williams Creek campground, and fish with that sharp and hungry edge of last outings. We sat around such a camp fire one night when an old gentleman came in, "hello'd the fire," sat a fireside log, and told us he'd fished the river way back, way back before the new road went in, said he used to cross the river and climb the big rock above Fairview and fish down from the far side. He had a gray beard and small blue eyes, was alone, and had driven up from California just to see the river one more time. I remember him very well. We were young, full of the present moment. He was old, full of past times.

Now it's myself experiencing what that old gentleman experienced by the camp fire, looking backward at this river, loving it, wanting to keep it. It feels like the memory of a bright steelhead. I hold it for a moment. I hold the river like a bright silver body, momentarily touched, fingers around the tail, under the belly, feeling that sinuous flesh full of life, vigor, and deep-sea memory. Then I turn it loose.

I turn it loose, but remember it, and that memory stays with me here on the North Bank affecting the ways I wade and cast, the ways I think, the ways I feel about these local rivers, and the way I feel about our North Bank house that stands overlooking the Rogue's shore. The codes and the values of the North Umpqua stay with me. So does the idea of how a river should feel and look. That's probably why I drive all the way up to Agnes and beyond sometimes, to find those bedrock ledges, and the tricky wading there that feels familiar.

At the present moment, here on the North Bank, I am watching gulls that have moved inland over the Rogue. They soar and beat and dip in the thermals, hundreds of them. Smaller birds, swallows probably, fly with them, all of them feeding on some hatch or other. I refocus my eyes to a closer dimension, trying to discover what the hatch might be, but all I can make out over the front yard are a couple of fluttering termites, what the locals call "red ants."

In the same way I look to the birds in the highest thermals, it is always tempting, when I think of famous rivers like the North Umpqua and the Rogue, to remember the distant dimension, the heroics of the legendary fly-fishers—those impossible wades, those incredible casts, those reservoirs of lore. But sometimes it's good to squint, to check out the close-up. A nice quality of the North Bank consists of the congenial ghosts just to the south, not an apple core's toss from our North Bank cabin's stoop, there at the now-vanished fishing camp of Rogue legend Glen Wooldridge. It's known locally that one time, when Wooldridge got around to washing out his underwear, he rather carelessly tossed it on a fence to dry, and one Mabel, who found it there and thought it discarded, cut off all the buttons to use in her sewing.

I knew Glen Wooldridge a little in his last years, and it's too bad I didn't know this story then about his underwear, because it would have been fun to kid him about it, and to hear what phrase he'd put to the event. He had a way with phrases that I liked, and I remember that when he spoke of his pioneering first run of the Fraser River Canyon, he did not say it was "difficult," or "dangerous," or "challenging," but said, instead, that it was "pretty snappy."

I like, too, that on this North Bank place we have an older cabin, a little like those abandoned ones on Grizzly Mountain. I don't mean our house itself, although it too is old and I often call it a cabin. This cabin I refer to is older yet, and out back behind the garage, with an apple tree on its west side, another apple tree on the east side, their branches meeting over the green-mossed cabin shingles. Only one original cabin wall still stands, with four eight-paned windows set into it. The roof rests on corner posts, shored up by the last owner who had a dog pen up there. There's a lot of slump to this old backyard cabin. The foundation posts and support timbers are pretty much gone.

Most everybody who has set eyes on that old cabin has asked me when I'm going to be tearing it down. But the fact is that I borrowed two big hydraulic jacks from Gerald Barton, who operates Barton's Body Shop over in Nesika Beach, and started jacking the place up. I did this with some care, listening to the timbers groan, then rolled around in the dirt under the corners poking at timbers with an ice pick. I'd never really seen the work of termites, or of dust beetles before, inside-out workers digesting the heartwood core of things.

Gerald Barton's father had lived in a trailer just down the hill from this place, and Gerald knew this old cabin from years back, when "Doc" somebody lived here and kept his collectibles in the old place—a dentist's chair, for one thing, and an old potbellied stove from a railroad car. While I jacked up the corners and ripped out the rotten wood, I thought of that old dentist's chair and how it would have looked. I wondered if Doc had come up and sat in it sometimes, looked out the eight-paned windows at far-off Kimball Bend of the Rogue, and recalled the teeth he'd pulled from one human jaw and another.

I cut new support posts from some discarded guardrail timbers, pried around the old concrete piers and leveled them out, used some more rough-cut lumber I found in the garage for cross supports, cut a couple new risers and built some stairs, glazed a few new windowpanes, patched up the cedar siding of that one wall, slapped on some paint, and the old cabin stands. The slant rain blows through it still, of course. But it's a good enough place yet to stack firewood. I like the homestead feel it adds to the North Bank, the flavor of early-times Rogue.

So the Rogue feels more like the home river, like marked territory, with each new foundation post under the old cabin, and with each new board of tongue-and-groove knotty pine that stands vertically into paneling in the back bedroom of the house, and with each new path discovered down a ferny bank to a riffle of the river and to a cluster of boulders where the otter climb around with their whiskers twitching.

I haven't fished the North Umpqua in three years. If I get up there this March, as I hope, I wonder if it still will seem anything at all like the home river. It's hard to think so with so many things changed, with so many details forgotten, with so many impressions of these coastal streams more fresh in my mind. It all makes me feel sometimes like a strayed steelhead half-pounder, nosed up the wrong river mouth, a little confused, pushing up past Elephant Rock to Johns Hole. The local steelhead do stray a lot, and it's not unusual at all to catch a Rogue-clipped steelhead in Pistol River or in Hunter Creek, say. I imagine, when that happens, those strays must rearrange their landscapes in a process somewhat like my own.

At any rate, those cabin pictures in my study hang there to remind me of all this. I suppose whoever lived in those sagging cabins, on the slopes of Grizzly Mountain, might feel the same confusion if they returned, might misremember the windows, the chimney stone, might forget just whoever it was that sat in that oak chair now three-legged in the side yard. Or if "Doc" came back to the North Bank, he'd not find that dentist's chair of his swiveling north to south along the view line of the distant Rogue. He wouldn't find three walls of his cabin, either.

Home ground or home water, they're both tenuous and fragile places, but I like to think we can take some of their essence with us, the way I dug some jonquil bulbs once from beside a cabin wall on Grizzly Mountain, carried those bulbs away with me in my backpack, and planted them elsewhere, or the way I cut buds off an old homestead apple tree not long back, up by Dunkleberger Riffle, and grafted them to a tree here on the North Bank. Those buds, a couple of them anyway, have swelled, bloomed, and grown sweet apples. Those splices of old wood to new wood are so smooth that the bark hardly ripples where the stocks meet.

I walked down to the Snag Patch this morning and looked at the brown flow of the Rogue. Two inches of rain fell yesterday, more the day before, more this afternoon, more coming tomorrow. The deadfall in midstream, my depth gauge, looks completely covered, invisible to the eye, not even a ripple to mark its underwater presence. There'll be a steelhead run or two come up the rivers with this water-surge; that's a fact. And the hard part will be figuring just where to fish, and when to get there, because these winter-run fish don't stay long.

Like some of the rest of us, they move on through, snuffing for some home-scent, for some feeling that is right, primitive, youthful, remembered dimly, all but lost, and needful to be found again before the water changes.

∾

Two

Neighbor S. gave me directions to his favorite upstream fishing spot, a place you can pull on down to with a pickup if you know the way. I drove up there one afternoon, just to see what it was like, bounced out through a lot of holes, drove out over a lot of stones, waded out and fished it a bit, but mainly it was a bait-hole, not much of a fly-drift to the place.

Since I was out fishing, though, and halfway to Lobster Creek, I thought to try a place my other neighbor, Neighbor J., had told me about, up above Lobster Creek Bridge. I drove up there, drove out along the Silver Creek Road for a piece, where it runs along the high north bluff of the Rogue, parked under a big pine, hiked up the road a ways, then skidded down some long, steep banks on sundry deer paths to the river, hiked up the gravel bar there, found what I thought was the place, and fished above the drop where the water slowed.

Below me on the river edge sat a guide boat, pulled over, camp fire going, smells of frying fish drifting towards me. The two old fellows and their guide sitting on the bank decided to show me their fish box full of bright chinook salmon and a couple smallish steelhead.

I fished down past the trio, through the drop, on into the riffle, and found the half-pounders, one on every cast. After landing six or seven, tiring of that, I walked on down to the drift above the bridge. I'd never fished there either, but often had seen the guide boats working it as I drove one way or the other across the bridge.

Two hats lay on the beach, sodden and green with weed, blown off some Mail Boat tour, probably. One read "John Deere," one read "Kiewit Pacific."

Willows grew thick at the top of the drift and forced my backcasts high as I laid out a couple of short casts, then a couple of longer ones, the sky getting dark, an upstream wind plucking at my rod and throwing loops in my line, shoving the fly upstream, making me mend hard to straighten things out some, but I enjoyed the smooth, steady, promising drift of the place, took a step downstream before lifting the line, and the fish hit.

It was a good fish, a jumper, jumping all over that drift, running to both sides, then down, then back up, then jumping some more. I towed her into shallows, pulled out the fly, pumped her in the cold water, thought she'd go maybe six pounds, firm and fat, sea lice still clinging. And I had to admit she was a better fighting fish than many an Umpqua ten-pounder, saltwater energy still bursting in her.

There was no one there but myself under a gray-dark sky, one star glimmering through a clear patch off to the west, the water numbing my hands in a way that made the rest of me feel intensely alive. When I relaxed my fingers from their hold, I felt the swish of the hen's tail across my hand. I stood there a moment, after she had flashed away, thinking how fish like that were the stuff of Rogue legend, then crossed the beach to timber, everything dark in the timber, and followed my feet, one arm bent, fending off branches, and scrabbled through blackberry, up over logs, slogging up that steep hillside. I finally found roadbed, high up, under moonlight. That steelhead, and the climb down and back to hook her, I remember well.

∿

The second one hooked up on a winter morning. I'd driven south to the mill, and pulled in. The man there, foreman or owner I gathered, said, "We're going to have to rent you a space." I'd been there a few times before. His two young daughters played with a duck decoy between piled slabs of burl. The smallest came over to me as I pulled on my waders and said, "We're going to have kittens."

"That sounds nice," I said.

Then her face turned away, her tiny finger pointed for her sister to see, and they both ran off to meet a small black and white dog that had wandered in from the highway along the mill road.

The water was clearing and down. The day before I'd fished below 101, the surf pounding, the tide out, and caught nothing. But a fellow had pulled in and parked beside my car, as I was putting my gear away, and said he'd just seen a steelhead go over a riffle above the highway, had cast some eggs at it, hooked it for a moment, then lost it. "You know how that is," he'd said, a young fellow with curly short hair, looking down at me from the high seat of his Dodge Ram. "No fish down below?"

I'd shaken my head. He'd looked perplexed, as though not believing it. "You just fish here, or all the way down?"

"All the way down," I'd said. But there'd been footprints in the mud ahead of me, fresh. Whoever had fished the morning flood perhaps had done better.

Whether it was that sighted fish, or the knowledge that other steelheaders were working the creek, or just the knowledge that the creek mouth had washed more clear and straight in the last torrent, a better passage now, I don't know; but gearing up there at the mill I believed there would be steelhead in the upstream pool I knew about. It was deep and narrow against ledge rock, a perfect holding place. Never mind that I had fished that pool the whole winter season without luck. I had a feeling, waded carefully, ducked crouching into the bushes and around the pool through blackberries and alders, upstream to a gravel bar where I could throw a short cast.

I dropped a big saltwater fly—orange, yellow, and rusted from salt, but a glittering sharpened point to it—down into the pool, jigged it around in the chalky green but couldn't get it deep. In a vest pocket I found a heavily weighted fly some friend had tied and given me. I'd caught steelhead on it, still had it in my box, and tied a careful slip loop, circled it over the fly, snugged the loop tight, and cast. The new fly drifted down along the ledge rock, nothing. The hope drifted out of me like smoke, and a cold wind started blasting up the creek, chilling my sensitive ears.

I moved to the base of the pool and cast back upstream, nymphing it, throwing some upstream coils, and reached for some pussy willow, pushing the soft catkins into my ears, the way I do sometimes when the wind gets cold, holding the rod recklessly, when the fish struck, my pose perfect Rockwell: fish on, rod slipping, finger in the ear.

The steelhead raced once around the pool, then down towards me, jumped a high flip-flop, landed with a splat, and I looked past it, to a break in the blackberries, and the two little sisters, black and white dog between them, watching and waving.

Two

The hen stayed in the pool, fearing the shallows below, I suppose, and made short, tugging runs, and a series of high jumps not much beyond the tip of my rod. Not wanting her to tire too much, I horsed her toward me on the heavy tippet and soon had her tail in hand, the leader also, and lifted her, looked at her, a perfect fish, fat and beautiful the way fat is beautiful on a fish, rounding the curves, without a scar on her, mirror-bright, and about eight pounds. She tugged and squirmed, the fly snapped off in her mouth, and I released her tail. She fell free, darting off without hesitation. I stood for a moment, watching where she had gone, watching to see if she would run out of the pool. She didn't, but went back down to the deepest part, hidden there in the green water along the ledge rock.

Two locals in plaid shirts were just heading out to fish as I came back to the car. We looked each other over, and I thought maybe I'd done that upstream hen a favor, and the creek, as well. She'd be ignoring flies or eggs or worms or spinners now, for a day or two, at least, plenty of time to get her safely up past the road heads, past the mud-wallowed jeep tracks, and on into the deep and roadless spawning canyon above. I remember her silver sides there below me in the cold water of that creek, and the mill owner's two daughters waving.

~

It is odd how certain fish stay very bright in one's memory, while others dim and grow distant. These two made their impression somehow; something about the weather, or the water, or the sky, or the particular thoughts of the catching-moment creased my brain deeply with memory, and stayed there. The two memories have taken their place, for the moment, among those that come first to mind when someone says to me "steelhead" or "winter fly-fishing" or words to that effect, or when I myself think in those terms. Then all the other river memories, the other fish, the other casts, come along afterward, as though they were all subconsciously ranked and filed, and required to wait their turns. Each time I go out fishing again, searching the riverscape again, the memory-file ranking opens up for revision, of course; and this opening again, this revising again in some shadowy linkage with memory, is part of the pleasure, I think, and part of the necessity. It's part of the framing of the mental map, too, that contours the North Bank country for me. But I do not kid myself that this map will ever be completely finished, or the filing of images completely finished either, until memory itself, with its shuffling imperatives, fades out.

I don't know just how many fish Neighbor S. has put up in his freezer for the season, but quite a few, he tells me, and his memories go back a long ways, back to the hog lines across the river mouth, and those kick-'em-out-with-a-foot days of plenty, memories old and rough, certainly different than my own Rogue memories, but mine are not so bad either. I'll take mine, and keep them.

∼

Size

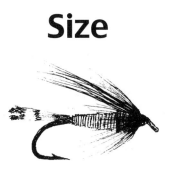

Early morning, rain pounding on the skylights, clouds gray, fog drifting up the valley, and I looked out to the east and saw blue herons, fifteen or sixteen of them, in cluster, slant down from their pine roosts and out across our road row of holly. They covered a good bit of vista, looked dark and ominous, like black horsemen of the sky, setting off for the wet hunt, four or five of them dropping down to the Snag Patch, the others crossing the river, bill-lances sharp and poised. Something about the numbers impressed me, the army of them like that, the size of their collective hunger. High as they are in their back rookery, they can drop down to the river with hardly a flap, just a kite-angled set to their wings, and a jet-nosed thrust to their heads. They're big birds for a fact. Sixteen of them could cover the sun.

Two weeks ago, myself down in a creek bend, an egret rose up through the alder, wings spread, filling the void between branches with a formless, tree-broken white, looking almost ubiquitous, merging with cloud. That's a big, dreamy, stilted bird, too.

Or not so many weeks ago, the mistake made of staying too late, casting, at Johns Riffle, after that fallen-light strike on the Street Walker, I felt my way north in darkness along the Snag Patch shore, stumbling into beaver channels, silt sometimes up to my knees, looking for the one lone crossing, startled suddenly by the slap of a beaver tail on the water, and the clatter of branches over my head as four night-herons launched out, clucking like chickens, the sounds big enough, made bigger by darkness.

At this moment, now, our cat, Sundae, is sleeping beside me, curled up in her Harry & David's Royal Riviera Pears box, with a paw over her eyes. She makes such a gentle snoring that I hardly notice it at first, then think it the weather, or some sound from the road, only realize it is Sundae by cocking one ear past the table down in her direction and seeing her belly rise and fall in synchrony with the sound, such a small catlike sound. Or there is the wren in the bush by the mailbox, a wren that makes—I think it makes—a tiny flicking sound of feathers as it twists and bobs.

These small sounds, almost too soft to hear, heard some sunny midmorning by the mailbox or in the warm security of walled ground, hold no comparison to cold stream clatter in the night of big wings beating branches, or beaver tail slapping black water, or to the ominous proportion of those spread-winged, floating forms of the herons. Looking out at the river from this cabin, this place of small sounds and safe creatures, seeing the heron brigands setting forth, remembering the chilled heart-drop of feeling in the Snag Patch dusk, I crave connection to that larger, darker energy. After a little easy chair and hearth I am ready again for the push of the river. I remember that a man with a silvery steelhead on his line can look across his shoulder and see the day's shadow pinned against a rock. I remember that oddity of Eskimo memory maps, the inaccurately enlarged home ground, and wonder how that happens, sure that it is happening in some subtle way in my own memory, pushed on by the herons and the beavers and those monumental winter storms out of the south, but pushed on, too, I expect, by the aggregate size of the tiny sounds, the mantra of purrs and flutters.

I have heard of those fly-fishers who fish for minnows, with tiny flies and three-foot rods, taking their pleasure from an accumulation of types, the way birders fill in their lifetime species lists. Certainly the small trout on the small stream has its beauty and its moments. I have felt them. If I lived in Wisconsin again, or in Connecticut again, places I have lived and fished in the past, the fourteen-inch trout would seem monumental, the eighteen-inch trout gargantuan, and all the proportions along the scale would adjust to the habit of those places. But here on the North Bank, with steelhead in every river now, the water murky with winter season, steelhead season, I can only think of the ironheads, the big dimension. Only yesterday Bob S., who runs a STEP (Steelhead Trout Enhancement Program) operation south of our place, told me his river was full of late-running steelhead, just come in on the last storm. "Seems like everything's running late," he said. "Hell, we had some fresh chinook come through in January. In January, now. That's just plain unusual."

I can feel steelhead moving in the local rivers, sense them in my blood. They are sometimes vaporous types, hard to find. But I try to match my sense of them with an occasional reality, as though leading to shore some heavy silver-sided fish fills in a negative form of fish already sketched in my mind, already real in the world of the North Bank, but requiring that validation of the catching act and the witnessing eye.

A day in February, then, the country an Irish-hills green, even the edges of Agnes Road mossed out to the tire track, and I drove up the Rogue to a place above Agnes where three pickup rigs stood parked along the road with bumper stickers like "Save an antelope. Bag a Bhagwan." I thought they were anglers, and the place crowded, but walked back along the road to have a look, couldn't see anybody below, and the riffle running clear enough to fish.

There should be a steelhead in there, I thought, and jogged the grassy road down, feeling excited, jogged the path through blackberries and myrtle, cut back west, slowing, cut across coon tracks, cut along the gravel to where the water began to pour and wave in the drop, then on beyond to where the current slowed to a bubbly smooth drift, and picked out a red and white fly I'd just tied up, head cement still curing, smelling strong and gluey in the fly box.

Alternating upstream and cross-stream casts, I worked my way along that drift. The wind gusted upriver so hard I had only to lift my line to mend it, and gusts sometimes grabbed my rod like a strike. When the real fish struck, it was different, though, a deep and sudden power, frightening for an instant. I thought maybe I had hooked something other than a steelhead, a seal maybe, or a sea lion.

This riffle in the runoff of winter pours for about two hundred yards before the river bends, and the fish ran deep into my backing and almost to the end of the riffle before it jumped. I could scarcely credit how far it had run below me, and then it ran again. I stumbled along over the rocky shore taking back what line I could. When the fish finally stopped, the line came back easily enough, the fish holding steady in the current along the base of the far bend, but so much line out, things so hard to gauge and measure, that it felt like a whole cat's cradle of line zigzagging in the current.

The big saltwater reel I was using held a lot of backing under the line when I started, almost all of it spooled out by that big steelhead. I kept running and reeling, and thinking the fish would be rested for another run if I didn't get down there faster.

The fish did run again, further down, then back up, which saved me breaking off, then down again, and another jump, then a series of short runs as I got it in close, but it had tired. The long-line game was over, the short-line game commenced, but did not last for long. When the fish rolled sideways, I saw its size, and tried once to tail it, but it bent my rod down against the gravel and almost broke it with a final burst of power. At last, I opted to pull the fish smoothly up on its side into the shallows. The barbless hook came out with one turn from my fingers. I put a hand under her, kept hold of her tail, and carried her back into the river, worked her upstream into the icy water, and looked down on the broad, speckled back, the sheer size of her.

Her nose came just lag of the thirty-eight-inch tape on my rod butt, and she felt as thickly muscled and heavy with eggs as any hen steelhead I'd ever held. Three scars along one side, and a ragged ventral fin just below the scars, showed some encounter, drift net maybe, her sides very bright, and her back a sea green.

She moved her tail, but I held her, pumping her. She tried again to go, but I held and kept pumping. She tried again, and I released her, felt her body flick against my fingers, watched her veer sideways into the current and away, disappearing, then saw the otter, just below, porpoising upstream.

The big hen was tired, spent, and needed to find some soft current to pour through her gills and revive her. All those dodgings and driftings of the juvenile, all that sea voyage of the adult, all this upriver journey, heavy with eggs, I did not want to end there, chased down and hauled to beach by the otter that kept porpoising, then cut out to midstream and dove. I picked up some rocks and waded deeper into the river.

The otter surfaced. It looked over at the screaming, splashing figure of myself, swam toward the opposite shore, dove a second time. For some minutes I stood watching, scanning the near shore and the far shore, expecting the otter to surface. It didn't surface. I lobbed a couple of rocks, and never saw the otter again.

If that hen survived, and I think she did, she laid a lot of eggs. I imagine her surviving, and she fills in a whole river of my mind with eggs, alevins, smolts, ocean voyagers, returning adults—silver-sided, powerful, so that a spawning of mental forms occurs right there in the gravel of my brain.

A few weeks later, the season winding down toward March, wood stain curing on the paneling project, I threw my "Spirit" hard-shell on the car roof racks and headed north, not really sure where I was going. But the Rogue was too rained-out and roiled for fly-fishing.

Down near the end of a river road, out where the country flattened to meadow, I pulled over at a gate, went through, walked over the grassy flatlands toward the river. The grass ended at a rock face dropping to the river, and the river flowed high but clear. I looked down at its green-pebbled bottom, searched for fish, thought I saw one, but changed my mind, moved my eyes downstream, and saw what I looked for, but a dimension that surprised me, so large I thought it might be an early spring salmon. I watched to see if it would move, the way salmon move, but it held steady, a steelhead then, exactly in the center of the river, on the near side of a rock.

It was an old routine: look down on the monsters, always in impossible places to fish, and try for them anyway. At Upper Redman on the North Umpqua I got one to chase my fly once, got it to chase halfway across the river from its lie against the far wall, my friend Wayne up in the rocks, calling the casts, but it never took, and that's about as close as I've come with any of the behemoths that I've seen from the start.

The fish below me held not far below a long rapids, not very difficult to get down in a kayak, from the looks of it, but hard to get back up, not much in the way of eddies on either side, and myself out of practice in the kayak, the hamstrings tight, the lower back tight. I did not want to press my luck too much, alone in a snowmelt river, but that fish was down there.

Another half mile upstream the road came back down to the river. Sun was warming things up. I pulled on a wet suit, waders over that, strapped my rod case on the kayak's front deck, dropped an extra roll of leader, a clippers, and a couple of extra flies in my wader chest pocket, then stepped into the kayak, hips too tight in the seat-padding, wading sandals too long for the foot room, and pushed off. But I headed upstream, getting the feel, and paddled up to the next rapids, got out stiffly, awkwardly, wave-wash rocking the kayak, made some casts, then paddled across the river and fished the far side. I fished it until I felt looser, then waded in to shore and put my heels, one by one, on a deadfall, stretching out my hamstrings. If the big steelhead had seen me looking down, and they generally do, maybe this one would have settled some in this interim and forgotten.

The chute-run went fast and easy, steadied on a brace, and remembering the form of that huge fish, I felt my stomach tightening. I didn't have a negative fish-space that large in my mental map of North Bank country. I nosed the kayak up onto gravel, walked along the graveled shore, and took some time to figure out just where the lie was, things looking different from the far side and from river level. A break in the fence on cliff-side opposite helped locate the place. But sixty feet of slack water circled at my feet before the center current. The river bottom pitched deeply down from shore, no place to wade. Willows, inundated by the high water, stood out from shore several feet, catching my casting coils. There was no way to get a decent drift, but, instead, just a short circling of leader, as though the fly were the moving foot of a small compass, the rest of the line mired in backwater.

Being down there, though, I saw another riffle below, fished it, and saw another riffle, walked down to that, two wood ducks flushing up off a side channel, and hooked a nice steelhead, a properly sized steelhead, just for an instant, before the fly pulled out. The fish came sideways, like a silver ingot, taking the fly. The reel ratcheted a couple of spins, before the weight released, gone, and my fault, too, that it happened that way, because I could have waded a little deeper, mended a little better, brought the fly through more slowly. But I hadn't done those things, thinking too much about the big steelhead upstream.

Estimating size is a risky process. Rule of thumb with steelhead holds that twenty-six inches equals five pounds. Each additional inch adds one pound. By this measure, a thirty-inch fish weighs nine pounds, a thirty-six-inch fish weighs fifteen pounds. The method can be off the mark by considerable, however, particularly with bigger fish. A spawned-out, thirty-six inch fish might weigh twelve pounds, or a really ripe female of that length might weigh eighteen or more. The system leaves a little room for poetic license. Girth measurement systems make for more exactness, I'm told, but I've never bothered much with those.

I spent some time fishing the Kispiox River of British Columbia back in 1976, trying for one of those fabled silver horses, and met Karl Mausser up there, whose thirty-three pound Kispiox buck still stands as the fly-caught world record. He knew there were bigger steelhead in there to catch, everybody did, and continued fishing the Kispiox every year, trying. Nobody was catching anything but sea-run Dolly Varden when I was there, though.

I met a man up there from Medford, Oregon, by the name of Marvin Darby. He said his dad "never knew a stranger," and trying to be like his dad, I guess, he invited our family to stay at a cabin on his ranch. Every day he'd ask how I'd done with my fishing.

Marvin was a carpenter. He claimed he'd looked at more than enough four-by-eight sheets of plywood in his day to have those dimensions memorized. He'd hooked a steelhead in the Kispiox a few years back that looked to him to be as long or longer than the width of a sheet of plywood, forty-eight inches.

"Had it right down at my feet, but I couldn't get that fish banked. He snapped right off."

Marvin liked telling the story, told it with loving detail, planed the edges of it smooth, brought the angled cuts to a perfect face. As he told it, my mind drifted a little to trying that British Columbia country on for home size. It didn't feel that comfortable. It had all kinds of wild beauty and space to roam, had rivers, mountains, wolves, and bear, but didn't quite contour to the ideal spaces of my thought. I liked more clearings. I liked more old barns, fallen rail fences, paths from place to place, and fish that measured some shorter than a sheet of plywood.

I think back in my own lifetime of fishing, think back about size, remember a few lunkers, but remember, too, that a lunker, for all its fable, is sometimes not the finest fish to catch. The first really big northern pike I caught was like that. The handle of my casting reel came off in my hands while I played that fish, and it didn't matter. He wasn't going anywhere, not doing anything much but shaking his head. And the biggest cabrilla I ever hooked in Baja practically beached itself, twenty-odd pounds of pure docility. Half the meat wasted, too, before I could eat it all.

My father caught a trophy muskie once, back in Wisconsin, a very long fish. He salted down the head and nailed it to a wall in our Milwaukee basement. For awhile he told me simply that he'd caught it, but then one day laughed and admitted he'd really netted it. It had been floating on the surface of the lake with a smaller fish stuck in its throat. It was a muskie over forty inches, however come by, and for several years the head smiled a predatory grin at everyone who descended our basement stairs.

Salting the big pike and muskie heads was a ritual of the Wisconsin-Minnesota northlands where I spent the summers of my youth. Hardly a ripe fishhouse stood that didn't have its row of salt-crusted pike skulls over the doorway. They were toothy and elemental. I always liked them.

"Stuffed" fish, as the locals call those mounted trophies in their dens, always seem a trifle sad to me, too close to real without being real. Better than stuffed I like inked, the way North Bank neighbor J. does it, a onetime Rogue guide who found his customers liked a rice paper trophy they could take home without dry ice. Using that ancient Japanese technique, *gyotaku*, Neighbor J. makes prints he displays and sells all up and down the coast. Last I talked with him he'd moved on from inking fish to inking spiderwebs.

No true stuffed fish has ever graced my walls, but in one corner hangs a stuffed paper fish fashioned by my daughter, Jennifer, when she was young and fanciful. It's big enough for any trophy, some four feet long, with terrible fangs, a body crisscrossed with purple and pink crayoned patches, some scales drawn in near the gaudy yellow tail, a trim of staples holdings its puffy bulk together, and a legend printed in bold letters near its belly: "BIGGEST BADDEST CARP!"

I'm told that fall chinook on some north Oregon coastal rivers run to eighty pounds. I'm told that they simply lie on the bottom when they are hooked, and after a bit decide to go back downstream, back out to sea, beyond bank following. The angler simply points his rod tip after them and waits for the pop. I'm told fall chinook on some south Oregon coastal streams on rare occasions go sixty pounds, a few forty-pounders each season, and occasionally get landed on fly rods. I don't try for them often. I did hike down to a river mouth last November, pursued by a pack of dogs, and cast for an hour before tide ebbed and the 4X4 crowd rolled in over the firm wet sand of the beach. The fall chinook that surprised me with a take last fall on the Rogue, just upstream from Lobster Creek, was a small one, comparatively speaking, somewhere in the sixteen-to eighteen-pound range I judged, a size that seemed perfect to me.

If I wanted nothing more than size for size's sake, I'd head down to a train crossing some blowsy midnight and cast to a passing freight car, get a quick screaming run that way, and break off. If I wanted nothing more than size, I'd have stayed out at Nesika Beach with my eyes on the far horizon of the Pacific. Dimension has its complexities. Size, for all its allure, has its limitations. The salted muskie head in the basement is only bone, like those village bone-beaches of Baja tumbling with the round bleached vertebrae of sharks that ultimately merge and crumble with the sand.

And what about cumulative potential? What about those chinook fry in the Coy Creek hatch boxes, hunkered down in stones? Last I'd been up there on my bike they were hatched, tiny as tadpoles but with potential for the hundredweight, thousands of the little devils just buttoning up and learning to feed, tiny hogs in the making. John Wilson had bucketed them up into Eskimo coolers and set up a scuba rig to bubble oxygen to them as we drove upstream in his truck. An Ophir school bus followed with a load of kids who had studied the salmon cycle. At the first stop on Euchre Creek the kids took turns carrying buckets of fry down to streamside, kept putting their hands into the buckets, feeling the slippery bodies swim through their fingers. The kids carried the most of them down that way, accidentally dropped a few flopping little bodies onto the truck's tailgate, scooped them up again into their fingers with words like "Wow-oh" and "Neat-oh," then pushed and shoved a little to get back into line and have one more chance to carry a bucket.

When that was over, and the school bus had pulled away, John and I hauled the remaining fry upstream another mile, backed down a muddy access road near an old camp fire pit, and emptied what remained into the creek. We held the coolers between us, turning them upside down, watching the tiny forms of black push out into the current together like ink drops, wiggle away to the first shore eddy, and hold.

It wasn't a big moment, but it was a home-sized moment. It felt right, and it felt good. It generated some feelings in me for the salmon of Euchre Creek and for the kids who studied them and hoped for their return. The whole day had a pleasant glow about it of accessible and reasonable dimension.

≈

Walking Back

Today I fished a local creek starting from an upper bridge and working down past my usual exit point, all the way to the mill. The creek was very clear, high, and fishless except for a couple of smolts. My usual way back is to cut cross-pasture and over-fence to a hole in the blackberries, slog upstream from there to an old road, follow that road back up along the creek to another pasture where the cattle study me with curiosity. At the pasture fence, usually with deer or bear fur in the barbs, I cross to the bridge where I've parked my car. But today I fished on down to the mill, convinced that with the river so fine, and the day so fine—sunny and warm—there must be a fish or two down at that deep hole just above the mill. There wasn't, and as I walked up through the mill yard, a worker in a blue shirt and with a short log across one shoulder came out a doorway and said, "Where are they?"

"You got me," I said. "I didn't see a fish or touch a fish. You seen any?"

"Oh shucks," he said. "I don't fish. I just like to eat 'em." And he went on by with a big spat-toothed grin.

I hit out up the road with my boot cleats clacking on the asphalt and a black and white pup of a sheepdog barking at me from across the road. I'd never walked back that way, and looked at my watch once to time how long it would take. The pup kept barking, and I asked him why, which he thought about for a low-yowling moment, before resuming the tirade. A kestrel kept flying-then-landing just ahead of me along the telephone line, taking off whenever I came abreast, only to land again on the wire just up the road. The bird seemed friendly. Its wait-then-fly tactics resembled those of our cat who sometimes streaks from bush to bush ahead of me across the yard. This kestrel even preened and fluffed with a feline aplomb. Some winter-coated horses jerked up their heads as I passed. A big red-tailed hawk soared to the north and screamed. And I saw Johnny M. up ahead leaning on his pickup.

His little gray mongrel rubbed its back on the truck bottom and half-barked with pleasure while we talked. "Oh he gets the cows," said Johnny. "He does that all right."

"Where you parked?" he asked then. "I'll give you a lift up."

But I said no, it wasn't very far, and asked him how he'd been keeping. Old Johnny has a thin gray stubble across his chin, a beat-over black felt hat, a few teeth across his bottom gums. He's up in the mid seventies, and when I say to him, by way of good-bye, that I'll be seeing him around, he always says the same thing: "Sure. If I don't kick the bucket."

He likes to tell me that he himself doesn't fish, has only caught one steelhead in his life. I ask where, and he points across his pasture at the creek. But I can fish his property anytime, he says. This, too, he says every time I see him, and always with the offer of a lift in the pickup sharing the front seat with the mongrel. I take him up on that offer sometimes, too, when time is tight.

First time we did that he dropped me at the mill with my car downstream at the lowest bridge, and he looked me up and down and said, "Where's yer boots?"

"These are my boots," I said, fingering my neoprene waders. I guess he'd thought they were some kind of fancy pants. He just shook his head, walked with me down to the creek, told me several times not to step in the muddy hole where they'd been scooping gravel, 'cause it'd be over my head, and said they'd used to swim here when he was a kid, and last year they saw three summer steelhead a-laying right in there where I was standing. Sometimes you listen to old Johnny, and you learn something like that, like summer steelhead where none are thought to be.

Standing there on the roadside with his mutt chuffing and rubbing, he told me about his tractors, one a '39 and one a '40. "Fired that '39 up just yesterday," he said. "Runs fine."

"That's the year I was born," I told him. And I said his place out back looked like it might have some mountain quail in the draws. Did it?

"Maybe a few," he allowed, "but there's too many bobcat around."

"You see them much?"

"Two nights ago was a cougar," he said, then some mumbled words I missed, lost in the tooth gaps.

"You saw it?"

"Right across the road. I was coming home from town, about midnight. They got him up on that hill."

He must have remembered then my newcomer status because he began listing off various cat-kills—lost lambs, lost calves. He'd called some friend with dogs, probably the fellow just up North Bank, across from the dahlia farm, whose dogs we can hear sometimes from our stoop when they get to letting loose in their kennels. Whoever Johnny had called had treed the cat and shot it. And just what Johnny was doing in town until midnight I have no idea. Spry as he is, nothing much would surprise me.

Taken all in all, this day of fishing hadn't been anything much in the way of catching, but the walk back, as so often happens, made up for that and left me with good feelings about neighbors and about their cattle and their dogs and horses, even about those fences of theirs that did not seem particularly aimed anymore at keeping me out. Then this mountain lion story that Johnny told—that gave me something to think about.

The North Bank environs are cat country from a long time back. Stories come in about the old days in the headwaters of the Chetco. That's a river in the south part of my mental map, one drainage north of the Winchuck. Naomi Cassel, a young girl in that country in the early 1900s, says the cougar and bear would kill ten head a night sometimes, that her dad one year killed sixty-two cougar and forty-two bear just trying to protect his livestock.

These days there're still quite a few cougar around, with sightings frequent and tracks frequent. I've found cougar tracks back on a sandy stretch of Geisel Hill, not a half mile from the North Bank cabin. So Johnny's news was no surprise. As I said good-bye to Johnny that day, and headed on up the road, clack-clack-clacking the cleats again, I wondered if this latest cougar-shoot would make the local papers. Probably not, though there've been a couple articles about cougar lately, a few cougar up by Agnes reputed to be following anglers along the riverbanks, never seen by the anglers themselves, evidently, but by some watching third person.

I catch myself wondering if I am one of those anglers who has been followed by a cougar, the whole affair watched by some curious third party at an overlook window of one of those Rogue cabins.

Most probably not, but the thought is arresting, and I wonder occasionally just what I would do with a cougar at close quarters. My friend Arlo up on Snow Camp Lookout Road, who had a big male cougar trapped and killed on his place after losing most of his sheep to it, assures me that a man wouldn't stand much of a chance against an aggressive cougar. He shook his head sort of quietly, too, when he said it, being no broadcaster of hyperbole. Thinking of that, I snap my delicate rod tip around now and then when I'm walking up a dark road, just to see if it would be of any use as a whip. It wouldn't.

As I walked on up toward the bridge, I planned in my head a spring trip up into some canyons, way on up past where I've gotten to so far, to see if there aren't some wild cutthroats up there that would rise to a fly. Plenty of cougar up there in those rock canyons, too, of course, but they should be fatted on fawns and sleepily tolerant by May.

I thought, too, at that moment, just how much of this fishing sport is the walking in, and the walking back out, particularly the walking back out, when the fishing rage is spent, the legs are giving notice, and the mind holds empty and full at one and the same time—empty of strain, full of the images of water, of current, and of sky, full of a growing familiarity with the paths and the places and the people who live there.

∼

One day on a small stream south of the Rogue, a drift boat crew pulled ahead of me in the riffle I had just begun to fish. They drifted behind me where I'd waded to midstream, then clanked out their anchor practically at my feet. Three spinning lines shot out over my drifting flyline. We fished like that for a minute.

I said, "If you don't mind my saying so, you guys could use a crash course in stream manners."

"We're just leaving," one said.

"So am I," I said, waded back to shore, and climbed up the hill toward my car without looking back. I was steamed. It was a slow, rough drive back out through the sheep gates to the blacktop.

I drove up the north bank road of that river and into the canyon where no boats run. I'd never been there before, had no idea where to go. The river fell away deep and distant, beyond sight or hearing, only a bluish valley curving east and south. I parked and scouted around.

The washed-out road that I found to hike dropped south, and pushed along through a series of gullies and blow downs. But it only looped me back, downhill, to the main road again. So I started straight down a wash, veered north when it dropped into a brambled gully, slid down into a creek bed, and realized this was worse than I'd expected. My feet kept dropping through holes. The hillside was unstable and running with water. Rotten logs broke and skittered ahead of me as I slid down a series of tiering banks. A grouse jumped up and settled down ahead of me beyond some ferns. Below me I could see glimpses of turgid river.

I reached the riverbank, jumped across boulders over a side slot, with crashing river drops above me and below me in a narrow, misty gorge. The rocks were wet and slick.

I wasn't going to make it back up that bank I had just slid down— too steep and long and gunky, crisscrossed with briar. So I hopped along over the boulder tops downriver, and saw a steep undercut cliff ahead, realized that if I'd slid down over that, I'd have broken some bone or other. An animal path ran along beneath the cliff. I followed down to another boulder field, and made a few casts there, but the water was too fast and deep, and the backcasts almost impossible. The further I went downstream, the less I would have to climb to the road, I knew, but my way dead-ended where a steep rapids cut against another cliff face.

Standing there, checking if there were a way to cross the cliff, I felt a memory surface from a black hole of brain—a time on the Umpqua when I'd tried to climb along a narrow down-slanting ledge some twenty feet above a pour-off. At the critical point a hornet had buzzed past my cheek. When I'd looked after it, up and to the side, I'd seen the papery nest, big as a melon, under a shady jut very close to my head. I wasn't sure if I could turn around, and didn't want to jump, but figured I could jump if they came. They were black hornets. My father had been knocked unconscious once by a nestful of them.

A cliff-hanging, black-hornet memory, not a bad one, either, as fortune had it. I couldn't think how I'd lost that memory, but was glad to find it again down in that canyon, and to integrate this river at hand with the Umpqua, and the stone of these ledges before me with ledge stone of old memory, and to get a little circuit board of connections going that gave me a boost of confidence just when I needed it. It made the imminent climb back look more possible, free of hornets at least. I found a cut-back path up over the first steep drop of bank, then pushed my way up high and higher through thickets, over and under branches, across gullies and seeps. Suddenly, there sat a sawed-off stump. Well, that's it, I thought; I've made it now. Somebody got down here with a saw. I'll just get through this slash and find the dozer track.

I was leaning against a dead tree trying to get my trailing foot over a branch, when the tree cracked and broke and I went backward down the hill and bounced onto my head and a shoulder.

But I only bounced once. The butt of my rod caught crosswise against a sapling, bent under me like a spring, and held. I scuttled my feet carefully over, around, and below me, and stood up—nothing broken, not the rod, not my head, neither leg.

The dozer track, paved with chips, lay just past the stump. I slogged the long way back uproad to the car thinking maybe a man my age ought to stay more to the beaten track, and then thinking what a bad sign it was to start thinking that way. Despite the bruises, this would all make a pleasant enough memory some day when I fished the lower river again and could remember that upstream canyon and how the water tumbled there. Despite the bruises, too, I had filled in another space on the mental map, shaped another negative space to real canyon.

~

I'd driven up along the Rogue the usual way, up North Bank to Lobster Creek Bridge, not quite sure when I started whether I'd stop at Kimball Bend or Lobster Creek, or go on up to Coal Riffle, or stop just short of there at Bradford Creek to fish a little riff I'd found above Fry's Landing, or hike down the road to Dunkleberger Riffle and wade the channel to the island, or pass by all of those places, for no particular reason, and head on up past the confluence with the Illinois to fish a couple of places I knew up by Agnes.

Why I end up fishing certain places instead of others I'm never quite certain. The better I know a river, the more subconscious the choices turn. Sometimes I pull over at a place without even thinking what I am doing, leaving things to a barely conscious choice, the way a person cuts a deck of cards, only half thinking about the ace, but a tiny voice inside saying, "Cut it right there." I realize sometimes that my mind is chanting a name as I drive east—*Dunkleberger, Dunkleberger, Dunkleberger*—cutting the river's deck for a feeling of luck.

This particular day I pulled over at Dunkleberger and walked the long curving jeep road down to the river, waded over to the head of the island and fished the length of the island without a touch, then fished a little bottom slick against the bank, rollcasting under the alders, and picked up six bright fish right there, one right after the other, cutting that river ace after all. Every one was a jumper, and every one I horsed in fast on the heavy leader, and every one had the hook in the jaw's corner and released easily.

Afterward, I waded back to mainland, pulled off my vest, peeled down my waders, and pissed in the weeds hoping a Mail Boat did not come by, but not caring that much if one did.

It was a fine bright day with a sky full of cloud shapes. The old apple tree near where I stood would be from some homestead or other, from a hundred years back. Its woodpecker-pocked trunk looked four feet around at the base, and a couple of rusted apples held high on one branch. The river out front ran rippling and filled with its memories, like a quivering muscle reliving an action. I stood there and felt the fishing fever lower some, inhaled the good air, and started back up the road.

The bear came from a bush almost beside me, sprinted down a gully in a black blur, and paused finally on top of the next rise. He turned and looked back, still close enough for me to see his eyes and his tongue, and the look of embarrassment he wore. We stood and looked each other over for a moment. "I jumped as high as you did," I told him. Then I walked on up the hill to the car and left him there, still watching.

On upriver I parked at a pull-off I hadn't tried before, and pushed down a ferny draw. The good water lay in a far channel. I struggled out, thigh-deep in fast water, to a shallower gravel bar midstream, and hooked three bright fish in a row, smallish but active, about twenty inches, then waded back and fished on downriver, happy to have discovered this new spot, still discovering and exploring. The holding-water soon dead-ended on an outside curve with the good water cross-river, a fine half-moon of gently riffling flow beyond my reach. What looked like a path led up toward the road but disappeared. I scratched the remaining way up a mud bank, then looked back and saw the house cross-river. It was a big white multi-storied place, and I thought, that must be the Lowery place, that must be Lowery Riffle on the far side, fished by many in earlier years at Lowery Fish Camp. Now I know where I am, and where Lowery Riffle runs.

It felt good seeing that house, feeling its ghosts, imagining all the seasons of steelhead on the lines of the Lowery Camp steelheaders who'd come down to the inside of that half-mooning riffle, waded in, and cast their lines to the drop of evening light. Standing high on the south road, looking out and across to the north, I realized that the river here looked different to me now, shaped and familiar and named. I walked back along the road thinking that, and thinking of the paths I'd found down through the trees to that gravel bar, and of its firm feel underfoot in the current.

On the back end of the station wagon, then, I sat unlacing my boots and remembering the day's action, knowing that when my wife asked about the fishing, I'd tell her first about that bear and how we both scared each other into jumping. Then I'd tell her about that big white ghost-building on the river curve, the Lowery place. That's the way I'd tell it, those things foremost.

$\sim$

Driving over from Ashland in March, I had my rod and waders in the back, and thought maybe some of the coast streams would be in good shape, falling from the recent rain, so I turned up a south bank road, drove around the curves, past the "No Trespassing" signs and the "No Hunting, No Fishing, Violators Will Be Prosecuted" signs, past the burned-out house, past the horses in their pasture with their blankets on, to the gate posted with two white signs:

WARNING
BEAR FOOT SNARE

DANGER—TRAPS
PELIGRO—TRAMPAS

with a yellow "NO TRESPASSING" sign between them. I opened that gate and went in, having a standing permission from the rancher.

The river was lower and clearer than I had thought, the gravel bar almost dry, only the far hole deep and green. But nothing took there, or on down below where I waded and walked. I'd felt one tap, and then lost the fly on an underwater limb that swayed and sprang with such a lively feel that I thought at first I had a steelhead.

I reeled in and headed back, cutting through fields towards the car, then stopped for a moment, just to see the place. My fishing fever was gone, the sun was high, the whole south hillside bloomed with daffodils behind rotten logs covered with bright green moss. Two does stood on the road above with forelegs poised and big eyes on me. A couple of lambs, just ahead, jerked on mama's teats from opposite sides, tails doing double-time, and mama nuzzling their behinds. Old hay lay thin across the greening field, and a lambskin lay torn and stained in the grass amid remnant offal.

All the bank-side alder were dropping catkins. An old alder in midmeadow, gnarled and gray barked, spread out like an oak. A myrtle thrust up beside it, round and green and full of yellow-streaked finches. The sheep bleated low, the lambs high, their shit stank and gleamed in the sun, and a lone ewe, off by the river, rubbed her side against a fallen tree.

The sheep let out more bleats when the rancher's blue pickup came rattling into view, down the road with a fresh load of hay, and pulled down into the field below where I'd parked. The rancher had his rig down in 4X4 low and driverless when I walked even with it, him out back, walking behind its slow roll, spreading hay.

"Fishing's about over now," he said.

"I suppose," I agreed, because he was right, mostly right. But there were two weeks left in March before closing, and a few bright fish still coming in that I hoped to find. I didn't want to interpret his remark as a discouragement. I didn't care that much if I caught any more winter fish, but I wanted to go through the motions, and take in the vista of that landscape I shared by his permission.

He was still tossing hay as I drove uphill and east toward the gate. I saw him pull his gloves tighter and stop to look out across his fields, look out at that same view I'd just looked at—lambs and catkins, finches, daffodils and sheep shit, steep rock face across the river, and that March-hopeful sky above, blue and bright and open.

≈

44

Places to Quit

March turned out to be the last month of steelhead season, and a month when I remembered all the times in previous months I had meant to go out, and all the times I hadn't quite made it out, mired in house chores. I remembered all those times the water had dropped and cleared and I had planned on the next day for fishing, but a rainstorm had come up in the night, bending the pines and slashing at the windows, and, of course, washing the streams back high again and muddy. I had heard about the April runs in some of the smaller streams and wanted to try them, thought the season went that long. One of the guides had told me you could fish those streams in April, but the regulations read differently, when I consulted them, and the feeling of imminent closing, as March drew on towards April, left me wistful and hungry for river days.

Spring was a time over in Ashland when the winter hills greened up, and the flowering almonds led out with their arrays. Every year I lived there, for twenty years running, one last snowfall dropped on the almond blossoms, white on white, and the following week or so I would head back into the hills east of town, to the old cabin sites, and find the daffodil shoots coming up thick to each side of where the doorways had once stood. There was nothing quite like that on the North Bank. But March along the coast could have its moments, and I wanted every day of it, including the last.

The thirty-first of March dawned sunny and warm, the rivers clearing from a rain, and I threw the waders into the car, threw in the boots and vest and rod, threw in a banana and a bottle of drinking water, and drove south toward the mill, parked below at the bridge, walked upstream through the cattle pasture there with the pungency of cow pies steaming up from the grass, and the meadow full of white flowers. Nothing held in the usual holes. So I drove on upstream to the mill proper and parked. "Park there and I'll have to forklift you," the owner told me, grinning, one hand covered with grease and gripping a big truck wrench. I moved the car out back near the myrtlewood slabs, carefully straddled the car over a mud hole, got out with a little jump across mud and pulled on my waders and boots, threaded up the rod, tied on a heavy egg-fly, and headed out, wading crisscross downstream to a hole I knew, fished it, walked downstream to look into it, and there lay a big steelhead, holding down lower than I'd ever seen one hold before, below where I'd worked the fly. I backed up and fished over him. He wouldn't move to the fly at all, of course, having seen me about the time I saw him. Well, damn, I thought, not a good way to quit for a day, or for a season.

Quitting right is a kind of art, when all is said, learning not to be wistful in late spring about cabin-doorstep daffodils, or closing seasons, learning other reasons to wander the fields and the riverbanks. I have friends who can reel in their lines on a minute's notice, be it the end of a day or the end of a season, but that seldom happens with me, always the perfect slick around the next bend. I expect age will assist me with this quitting lesson, but it is not a lesson I want particularly to master.

Maybe it's the absence of a proper role model that encourages this intransigence in me. Back some years, in Wyoming, when the family camped at a certain lake in the Wind Rivers, my dad and I used to hike five miles or so to a brook trout stream, and somehow never quit fishing until dark. Part of the trail home ran through meadow along a feeder lake, and I remember seeing the outlines of moose against the red-black western sky. Then we would hit the timber. On moonless nights, ourselves always without a flashlight, we sometimes got down and crawled along parts of the path, feeling our way home with our hands.

Or out on Burntside Lake, or on any of umpteen-odd other lakes in the border country of Minnesota, with the three-horse Evinrude putting along on the back of a rowboat, we'd look north and see the black clouds swelling, feel the wind pick up, and we'd keep right on trolling, finally end up on some island shore sitting under dripping trees watching rain blow at us and the whitecaps pounding on shore rocks, feel raindrops running down our necks as we thought of those smarter folks back in their dry fire-warmed cabins. It always smelled fresh out there on those islands, though, fresh and clean and piney in the rain, with maybe a loon calling, and sometimes a few blueberries at hand.

When my mother went along on Burntside Lake, we always headed back in to shore at first sighting of the evening star. "There it is," she'd say, pointing. "Time to head back." That was a nice tradition, a sensible way to quit.

But when stubbornness gets rewarded, as sometimes happens, it only makes quitting the harder. One day on the North Umpqua, when my partners had quit, I kept going on a fishless morning and ended up at Cliff-Hanger, the last shaded place I could think of, my legs wobbly, sliding down the hill to the river, my body swinging out over space for an instant, hands around a tree, until the boots touched stone. From there it was an easy slide down rock face, a short upstream wade, and a climb across a log, to the casting spot. On the third cast, deep and unlikely, came that pull, then the long run and jump of a twelve-pound hen, one of the most perfectly beautiful steelhead I've ever landed. I held her there in that cool shaded gorge, pumped her, released her, then sat down on a stone, cut off the fly, and knew it was over, for the morning anyway.

Or all those evenings at Hayden Run, back when that slick was more or less a secret, and the fish came up out of the Station and the Glory Hole just before dark into that almost unnoticeable slick below the Sawtooth. I'd go down there the last legal minute, as everyone else headed back to their cars, go down there with barely enough light to cast, step down off the bank at the place I knew, wade five steps out on the ledge, climb up on a long flat rock just breaking the surface, edge up to the top of that, cast a whistling line in the semidarkness, out and across, feel dizzy over the dark white water, hook up, and hear the pawl-prayer spinning as darkness came down across the river. There was something exciting and elemental about the reel's spinning in the darkness, about that silver power out there in the black river currents, and about knowing I was out there alone, all the other fly-fishers gone back to the Inn for their dinners and their coffee and their day's tale-telling around the fire. Quitting early is tame and easy and sensible, but lacks excitement, risk, pain, and the black-river hook-up that sometimes happens out there on a lone ledge in a dizzying alter-plane of purple cloud, with the shuffling feet feeling along their ways at last to shore, and the blood pounding approval.

Other times at Hayden, though, proved less perfect, like the cold December afternoon when a sensible halt would have saved more trouble—after falling in first at Redman, off that deep boulder, swimming in just above the rapids, climbing exhausted and cold to the car, changing into my extra clothes, turning my waders inside out, and then going down to Hayden, wanting my boy David to catch a fish. I helped him move up behind me on the flat rock, leaned out a little too far to let him past, and fell in again, icy swift water sucking out my strength. David reached out his rod for me to grab. The tip pulled out, as I held it, and ran down the line to the hook that imbedded itself in my hand heel. It was a steelhead point of view I learned there, certainly, played into shore on a rod butt. The drive home was clammy and cold, my teeth chattering. It might have been better, taken all in all, to quit after the first wetting.

But you never know. If the darkest hour comes right before the dawn, as that old blues chorus has it, then continuance holds its promise. It's way too easy to think you can fish into April, and find yourself closed out at the end of March.

One time, one of those end-of-summer North Umpqua trips, Catharine said to me at the door, "Bring home a fish this time, will you? We've got that dinner party next week, and a big steelhead would be perfect."

It proved a trip when the vine maple glowed orange and yellow at the river edges, and the water flowed clear and steady, and frost shook off the tent each morning, and the river was full of bright steelhead, and the camp fire each night lulled us, and a fraternal bottle, passed about catching firelight, lulled us, and the river chortled and gurgled at us in the darkness like a baby.

It proved one of those trips when the quitting came especially hard, friends pulling in one direction, the river in another, and only that big fin-clipped buck steelhead down in Rip Rap Canyon, finally, that last morning, solving the issue, immolating itself, the sacrificial dinner-fish that I sat on finally, out there on the rock-cap island, to keep it from sliding back into the river, while good Jim waded out after me thinking I'd broken a leg. No need to keep a fish early, I'd reasoned, most of those I landed being wild anyway, then had to have that fish on quitting day. Bouncing back across the boulders to shore, water sloshing in over the waders, the steelhead towed behind on my wading belt, Jim out front leading the way, I felt like a strayed puppy being brought back to the family hearth, the car up there on the road all packed to go, tent stowed, sleeping bags stowed, everything ready to roll on home, everything ready but the compulsive one.

Changing the word itself might help. *Quitting* holds all those connotations of retreat and defeat, head-hanging, turn-tailed back treading; but, once re-creation happens, once the mind smooths out like a fresh sheet, re-creation as a process turns redundant. Then I should not say to myself, "Now I am quitting," but, "Now I am re-created and completed," and round out the fishing days with some circular memory, some integration of foreness and afterness. Saint Augustine believed that the presence of rivers proved the earthly presence of angels. I should remember that, and consider Augustine's angels re-creation enough.

On the Rogue now, North Bank country, my legs older, the boots feeling heavier, there is some physical pull for reform, but the mind resists my tricks of name. The round-it-off image, the merry-go-round of form, relapses to a linear bronc-ride to the buzzer. I stay down there at Coal Riffle into the long shade. I fished down one late evening toward two porpoising otter, and talked at them a little. "Get out of here. Give me twenty minutes. That's all. Go on across the river." My mind kept changing with each cast, thinking to make each cast the last, but the arm still moving, the line still arcing back and tugging and bending smooth and arcing forward. Finally I said it out loud, out into the the pour-off, *This will be the last cast, now, absolutely the last one.* The line arced back, then sucked in its belly and flattened forward, pulling the coils of running line from my mouth, straightened out, and still pulled, and grabbed another foot of line off the reel as the whole line hit its end point, and popped, and settled. The instant the fly touched water the steelhead hit hard, turned down into the current. Then stopped. Then took off again, and I pointed the rod tip downstream and broke off, nothing else to do, no place to wade downstream, no way to stop that fish. It gave me a great moment, a reinforcing buzz of prize for last-casting, and darkness is where I quit best.

So I didn't stop fishing on the thirty-first of March, because half a day of season remained. The legs felt tired a little, but the drive up to another river would rest them, I thought, and I cruised along the headlands, over a cape, the surf rolling and white. I parked behind a gas-groc, waded cross-river under a bridge and on upstream where I'd never fished before. The slow bubbly drifts looked fishy and right, with a lot of them to cover. The higher I went, crisscrossing the river, the better the slicks looked, a little more current to them, a little easier to see where a steelhead might hold. But nothing hit on my casts, and my confidence waned. I'd enjoyed the exploring, figured this new territory was reward enough for the drive, but then made one last cast.

The fish, probably a salmon, hit in a deep, slow drift past a sunken log. I never saw much of the fish, just one silver-copper flash. It fought on the bottom, heavy, shaking its head. About thirty seconds ticked by before the fly pulled loose, came in bent, skittering over the water as I reeled.

They would all come back around, some other time, I thought, all those merry-go-round silver ponies of the river, and the day felt warm and spring-like, and the season felt complete enough. I had found some springtime North Bank moments, made memories of them, some stubborn bronco memories of not-quitting, and it felt good to have some North Bank memories like that to put up on the same shelf with those stubborn Umpqua memories. God knows it's hard, though, to quit a river on a warm spring day.

I snipped off the fly, stuck it in the wool vest-patch, and reeled the leader in through the guides. Was I really quitting before dark? Would I really be back in time for dinner and World News Tonight? It seemed that way, and I cut across a field up to the road, and walked back along it, smelling the fresh new grass of the fields, my boot studs clicking on the blacktop under late-afternoon sun, and a red-tail peeling and circling off to the south, screaming its mouse-jumping *kreeeeeee*, that cry of won't-quit-'til-I-get-you hunger.

~

Silver Ponies

I joined the local chapter of STEP (Steelhead Trout Enhancement Program), affiliate of a group called Curry Anadromous Fishermen, and drove in to Wednesday night meetings once a month at Rogue Landing Restaurant where about fifteen of us would sit around in checkered shirts at a back room bar, drink a few beers, eat deep-fried chicken from a basket, listen to fish business, and harangue various government representatives. I'd lay my door prize tickets out flat on the bar and hope it might be my lucky night to win a pair of socks or a box of swivels.

During the week, I'd get calls to go out seining, and I'd drive on down to Hunter Creek, say, or up to Huntley Park on the Rogue, to join the hip boot crew, slide down some wet bank or other, and slither around in the river trying to seine out brood-stock salmon. Or sometimes I'd drive on up to Bark Shanty hole on Lobster Creek and watch ODFW folk in dry suits trying to drive salmon down into the nets. Three or four of us volunteers would stand along the riverbank shivering, stomping our cold feet, and holding various ends of the big capture net.

Also I signed on as a volunteer feeder/factotum at the Indian Creek Hatchery, Wednesdays my day to drive in six times, check oxygen levels in the tanks, and scatter feed out over the tank-tops to the growing chinook fry. Joining up for this sort of thing runs a little counter to my habits, but I wanted some investment in this North Bank country.

Wednesday morning, then, springtime, sunny and cold, the Rogue still high and dark from the previous week's big rain, but the water falling, the gauge-stump in the Snag Patch just starting to show, and I drove in to Indian Creek early for morning chores and feeding, rolled down the North Bank, crossed the Wedderburn Bridge, turned left on Jerry's Flat Road, turned right past the Pancake House, bumped over the cattle guard, and idled up Indian Creek Valley on Knox's private road. Myrtlewoods arched over the road. I looked for wild turkeys on the east hillsides. Sometimes they're there. The fields glittered with dew-green on the hillsides, shone with daffodils on the flats, a few cattle grazing, and a shit-hided bull stood head down beside the road.

The sun fell away to shadow as the canyon narrowed up ahead. The hatchery building stood in cold shade, and locked, with a green dip net still lying across fry tank C. The springwater that gets piped down off the hilltop was running clean and cold, no problems there. The key to the shed hung on its accustomed hook. I unlocked the door and went in, confronted the "Keep Out" sign and went past it, got the dissolved-oxygen meter out of its aluminum case above the sink, turned it on to warm up, and went back to the outer shed to make the day's communal pot of coffee.

Forty-four-thousand-some eggs had held in the incubator trays, stripped out of twenty-some female chinook this year, fertilized with milt from about forty males, three males to a set of eggs to increase genetic diversity. Forty-four thousand eggs was less than half the hatchery's capacity, but better some eggs, we reasoned, than the previous year's goose egg, when the netting for brood stock came up so empty that what we did catch we later released.

This year's trayed eggs have hatched, and most of the hatchling fry have begun actively feeding in the outdoor fry tanks A, B, and C. Six batches of eggs from late fish remain indoors in their trays, in the dark of the incubation room, gradually absorbing egg residue into their stomachs and "buttoning up." A few fish have died and float tail down or bulbous belly up. These are removed daily by various volunteers using a sieve spoon. A few other hatchlings have two heads and swim oddly. These get seined out, too. I have heard of the occasional albino, but have not seen one. A few very black hatchlings dot here and there in the trays, but these appear to be as healthy and wiggly as any.

The dissolved-oxygen reading for the outdoor fry tanks that February morning stood well into the green at 10.5 parts per million, same for the indoor trays. The water temperature held at fifty degrees, and the water of the tanks, like the creek that feeds them, was clearing up. I had a few "morts" in outdoor tank B, more than a few—sixteen. But we held almost eleven thousand fry in that one tank, so a few mortalities didn't flag anything unusual. The slack dead bodies, still intensely silver, I dipped out with the net and tossed across the road into the bushes, then recorded the number of morts on the tally sheet.

Time next for thermal-unit math.

Every degree of water temperature above freezing, per day, in whatever tank or tray is being monitored, constitutes one thermal unit. A fairly exact measurement of where any given group of eggs or young fish are at in their development can be calculated by simply summing these total units and comparing them to known totals. For example, at 450 thermal units chinook eggs eye, at 900 they hatch, at 1,665 the fry are fully buttoned, ready to be moved to the outdoor fry tanks, and ready to start taking fish food. So it is one of my jobs to record the temperatures of various tanks and trays, then add the thermal units to a running total kept for each unit.

The tray readings were all fifty degrees. I added degrees over freezing, eighteen thermal units, to the current sums, sipped my coffee, and wished I'd remembered to bring my reading glasses.

The thermal unit calculations finished, I opened the freezer, dug out some pasteurized fish meal, weighed out into separate containers the proper ounces for each tank, and went outside. It was warming a little, but the top screens on the fry tanks looked dew-wet. I slid them off, then flipped in some fish food with a seed-sowing motion, and watched the little devils rise.

It is one of the problems of fish culture that artificially fed fry gradually begin to associate overhead movement with feeding time, that they do not flee from it, but flock to it. The fry in tank C are still so spooky that the food I toss floats once around the tank before the fry settle down to feed on it. But the older fry, in tank A, already swim over to my side of the tank when they see me coming. Next July or August, down on a bay filled with egrets and herons, gulls and mergansers, this attraction to overhead movement will not serve them well.

Each week I see changes in these fry—growth, increased agility and speed, changing color and shape. Now when they feed, they do not wait for the food to sink, do not take it at midlevel or bottom level, the way they did at first, but shoot to the surface, sometimes over the surface, like a writhing mass of eels. When the fry were smaller, and less used to feeding on fish meal, some of them would hang vertically, tail down, under a particle, eyeing it. But that caution gradually gave way to abandon.

The fry grow as the season grows, but the drive in to Indian Creek remains the same, and the chores remain the same. There is no excitement involved, only the quiet satisfaction of feeling generally useful. The Wednesdays pass, turning round and round each week in the same way that the fry and the parr move round and round in their tanks, heads into the current that washes in a whirl. Their tiny silver forms, ponies in the making, ride their merry-go-round currents, and in the process reinforce that image in my mind, while meantime Knox's pretty-headed horses dance their springtime dances in the fields and amble over sometimes to the fence lines to have their soft noses scratched.

One morning as I drive in I have to chase turkeys out of the hatchery access road, two toms strutting for the hens, tail feathers wide, wingtips to the ground, wing bars sheening a bronzy green. I owl-hoot at them, and they gobble, then strut off up the hill behind their hens. I set about my business at the hatchery, taking readings, measuring fish food from the freezer. A peeping sound in the outer shed attracts my attention. The peeper turns out to be a hummingbird perched on the overhead fluorescent light fixture. It has gotten locked in the hatchery building somehow. It flies around the contour of the ceiling several times, obviously tired, worn from the ordeal. I try to herd it toward the open doorway, but it won't drop below the doorway header.

Exhaustion will claim it soon if I don't do something, it appears, so I get a dip net off the outer shed wall and catch the bird just long enough to drop it below the doorway header. When I shake the net out, the hummingbird buzzes away, peeping wildly.

A thoroughly birdy day—turkeys, hummingbird, buzzards up in the thermals. I stand there feeding fish, sowing food with a hand turned numb from morning cold and from ice particles in the fish meal, fingertips throbbing. I watch the silver bodies of the fry churn, rising up from the tank bottom like the bottom itself, like someone were tipping the tank on its head, all the contents spilling, all those quick, darting hungers of youth readying for sea.

It should be another day of satisfaction at a worthwhile task, but questions follow me along the walkways. Watching that hummingbird at ceiling level, unable to escape, has gotten me ruminating. A part of me remains a little skeptical about hatchery programs, about the easy assumptions in the undergirding. This Indian Creek program seems more sensible than most. But I question outcomes, crave exact answers about effects. I want to know precisely what we're accomplishing—here at Indian Creek, and on those other creeks; or just what the South Coast Fishermen accomplish with their projects on the Chetco; or what all those other volunteer programs along salmon and steelhead streams of the Northwest accomplish.

It's possible, it occurs to me, that we do-good volunteers are just another part of the problem, another contributing factor to fishery depletion, blindly making ourselves feel useful. That's not necessarily how it works, but it's a proposition to consider, and one made more immediate by the sometimes-worried looks on the faces of the ODFW staffers as we haul yet more brood-stock salmon from the creeks. The idea is made more immediate, too, by the occasional fish-kill accident at the hatchery, catkins and leaves blocking off some straining screen in the night, half the fish belly-up before the hatchery alarm activates and some volunteer tumbles sleepy eyed out of bed.

There are those people, a good many, who would build as many hatcheries as they could finance, capture as many brood stock as they could capture, raise as many fish as they could raise, dump as many fry as they could dump, thousands and thousands of fry, into every feeder stream of every major drainage. I heard those sentiments voiced, unofficially but forcefully, at a recent conference on the Rogue River and its future, held in Gold Beach. The season's biggest storm huffed along the rooftop outside, rain rattling, while inside the building resounded that medieval proposal of how to solve the Rogue's depletion. I drove home in darkness through a roaring wind. So many myrtlewood branches had broken, so many leaves been torn, that the whole town, the whole river valley, smelled of myrtlewood, a perfumed wind in a sparrow night, wild and strange, a night to humble human pride if we would listen to its music.

I got interested in the Indian Creek program when told that its purpose was to restore the Lobster Creek chinook, a late-running, deep-bodied fall salmon that used to keep local anglers busy in the lower Rogue well on through November. I'm not a salmon angler, particularly, but a wild run is a wild run. I figured the more such runs we saved, the better for the future. The idea, as I understood it, was to supplement the wild runs in Lobster Creek, Jim Hunt Creek, Quosatana Creek, until they once again became viable, then leave them alone, and work on stream habitat, and keep the whole system healthy.

Old Gene R., hatchery manager at the time, invited me into the hatchery shed, lit up a cigarette, and told me about it. Also he told me a few good places to drop a steelhead fly. "Hell yes, I've fished all over. Up in Alaska, too. Wish I could take you out."

That was some time back. Now Gene R. has a pig valve in his heart, and the hatchery has been built up—a walk-in freezer installed for food, new fry tanks installed and screened, new raceways installed and screened, a new holding pond constructed, a lot of money and effort put into improving a dual water supply, the building improved, a new spawning shed in the works, a parking lot improvement. It's big stuff, enduring stuff, things that lend themselves to permanence, long-term propagation, annual funding, self-perpetuation, copious volunteer labor, and even the occasional tourist tour.

A lot of hard work, money, and good intentions have gone into the building of the hatchery. There's a sense of civic pride about the place, personal pride too, and hope. I share a good deal of that, have invested more than fish feeding time on the project, and can claim, in a small way, a personally fashioned corner or underpinning here and there. But also I harbor these reservations.

For example, the Indian Creek Hatchery exacts a toll not only on the annual wild brood stock collected in various feeder streams of the lower Rogue, but on the spawning potential of Indian Creek itself. The upper spawning grounds of Indian Creek are dammed off in order to supply one of two water sources for the hatchery. State biologists want no upstream spawning that might carry diseases down to the hatchery, so there are no fish ladders past the dam. Indian Creek steelhead, a significant run at one time, have not much place to spawn unless they jump the dam, which some still manage. One stock suffers for the enhancement of another.

Then there is the matter of the fish themselves, their abilities to survive and spawn. My general misgivings about hatchery fish go back to the seventies and early eighties on the North Umpqua. Hatchery steelhead boomed there for awhile, then declined, taking the wild stocks down with them. Saving the wild run on the North Umpqua is now a major management concern of the ODFW.

The Umpqua got planted with exotic stock, fish from the Washougal, as I recall, a Washington tributary of the Columbia. The wiser Umpqua stocking program now underway, using indigenous fish for brood stock, may, or may not, increase the runs; but even if it does, the gene pool of the North Umpqua steelhead is inevitably narrowed by such programs, and the fish themselves altered.

Various studies of the last several years document what anglers have known for some time: hatchery fish are inferior fish. On the North Umpqua we called them "dogs," and with reason. They looked spawned out before they had spawned. I have hooked a lot of these fish over the years, fish that did not run out line, did not jump, did not do anything but hang in the current and shake their heads. Eight-, nine-, ten-pound fish, they were silver enough when landed, but bag-of-bones nags in the river, doing nothing at all exciting. Of course on the barbecue grill they cooked up nicely, and placed no hard demands on the conscience, either.

If someone wants to argue that catching an eight- or ten-pound steelhead should be excitement enough for most people, that the rating of fighting qualities is a pastime for jaded purists, that we can afford some loss of fighting qualities for the sake of renewed or sustained runs, I will agree. I will nod my head in affirmation. I understand those arguments.

But, there's this hitch. The same characteristics that make hatchery stock inferior fighting fish also make them inferior spawning fish. Studies show that the typical hatchery salmon or steelhead spawns at about one-eighth the efficiency of a wild salmon or a wild steelhead.

How can this be true? I wonder that myself, aware that there is hardly a "pure" wild fish left in our rivers and streams, almost all of them subject to plantings at one time or another. But small-time hatchery operations, like the one back in 1877 run by cannery owner R.D. Hume at this same Indian Creek site, were imbedded within a framework of copious runs, with a lot less genetic impact on the total populations.

"You can make these babies into anything you want to make them—big, small, wide, you name it. It's scary," says Dave Harris, local ODFW fish biologist. A couple weeks more have passed from that hummingbird-turkey-buzzard day, and he's out at Indian Creek weighing the parr, scooping them into buckets, putting the buckets on a scale, finding out how many parr to the pound. I'm helping him count the fish back out of the buckets, two or three at a time slithering in my fingers, flopping across my hand as I count them, dropping back with a flip into fry tank D. I've been asking Dave some things about feeding, telling him I feed the fish extra sometimes.

"You can get fat, lazy fish that way," he says. "That's my experience."

So I tell him some stuff I've been reading, how I got Mark Chilcote up at the state office to send me a short bibliography of the most pertinent studies about hatchery versus wild fish, how I've managed to get those articles through interlibrary loan, read them, mull over them on Wednesday mornings along the raceways while I feed the parr. I tell him—while he nods, knowing it all already—how hatchery fish develop smaller fins, smaller tails, longer and thinner bodies, narrower caudal peduncles, how they become, in short, less powerful fish.

All the studies verify that swimming power, "burst speed," is an important selector on natural spawning beds. Strong, thick-bodied fish with powerful burst speed, the characteristics of wild fish, make better redds in the gravel, defend those redds better against encroaching fish, and avoid spawning bed predators more successfully.

Using at least fifty percent wild fish for each year's hatchery brood stock, the policy at Indian Creek, certainly helps maintain those burst speed genes, but burst speed must play a role, too, in what wild brood stock we manage to net in those volunteer, hip boot forays.

Up on Lobster Creek last year, for example, I held one end of the net while two biologists in dry suits herded a big female chinook down into the belly of nylon. When her nose hit net, she exploded, turned upstream and was gone so fast, burst-speeding so fast, it was hardly credible. We settled for something slower.

In natural spawning conditions, the smaller eggs of wild stock seem to survive well. But again, without the natural selective processes, the eggs of hatchery stock tend larger. That's just another one of many variables that may account for the poor natural spawning record of hatchery fish.

A couple generations of hatchery propagation are all it takes, too, to effect some of these basic changes, to go from a thick-bodied wild fish to a lanky hatchery Frankenstein. It is very, very clear that significant numbers of wild stock will always be necessary as a gene repository, as a tonic for what biologists call "inbreeding depression." Without wild fish to use for fifty percent or more of brood stock, hatchery fish will soon lose those fundamental wild characteristics basic to survival in the rivers and in the ocean, and, if that happens, the silver ponies won't be coming around again no matter how many hatcheries we build or how many smolt we plant.

As for those who argue in favor of more hatcheries and more plantings of hatchery fish, they would do well to read the reports on what biologists call "density dependent mortality." River environments can support only so many fish. Go beyond that level of fish population and it is like putting too many elk or deer on a limited winter food supply. All of them grow weak, most of them die. With one hundred deer, say, yarded up in a place that can support one hundred deer for the winter, a high number of them winter successfully. With two hundred deer in that same deer yard, maybe twenty deer survive, those twenty in bad condition. More deer make for less deer, and less healthy deer, in the long term.

In rivers this phenomenon is less visible, but no less real. The Klamath is another river like the Umpqua where fish runs in the last decade fell victim to this kind of density-caused depletion. Pushed on by public demand, California fish and game biologists planted more and more hatchery fish in the Klamath; but the more fish they planted, the fewer came back, and in the process the wild stocks suffered enormous losses.

Even in estuaries "density dependent mortality" happens. The notion that we can leave the upper rivers for wild stock, plant the estuaries heavily with hatchery fish, and reap the best of both worlds, holds true only if those estuary plantings are very, very carefully timed. Recent studies document heavy density-caused mortality in estuaries. In years of poor upwelling, this kind of mortality probably occurs even at sea.

Typical hatchery programs show initial success. Fish populations explode. Everyone congratulates each other on jobs well done, with high-fives and cheers all around. Six, eight, ten years later, all that changes. By then the wild stocks have dwindled to dangerous lows. The hatchery fish have become more "inbreeding depressed," almost incapable of successfully spawning on their own. Nothing comes over the counting stations. Wistful hatchery and hatch box managers wonder where their babies have gone. Tourism declines. People get discouraged. Volunteer labor dries up for programs like STEP. Misinformation grows rampant. Local frustration turns to misdirected anger: it's all the fault of the Japanese, or of the Native Americans.

State biologists start cutting back on hatchery programs, realizing, finally, the negative effects. The public starts screaming for more hatchery programs, not understanding the sound reasons for the cutbacks. This uninformed public pressure, although understandable and well intentioned, simply politicizes the problems and makes them worse. The North Umpqua and the Klamath are only the most immediate examples of river systems overstrained by massive stocking programs. Wild coho salmon all across Oregon have suffered from density-dependent mortality, as have chinook salmon all across British Columbia.

If we've learned anything in the process, it's this: the hatchery factory must be subordinate to the river system, to what that system can sustain.

The hatchery solution, as a total solution, was a simpleminded myth from the beginning, but appealing. It dies hard. I stopped one day on the bridge above Agnes and talked with a river guide there, both of us looking down at the same empty river hole, searching for overdue salmon. "Shit," he said, angry. "Fire the goddamned managers and I could fill this river back up in a year, so many fish you wouldn't believe it."

"Sure," I said. "But what would you have in ten years? That's the test."

Think how much of the myth we've swallowed, how much we still swallow; think of all those dams without fish passage, the lost upstream habitat balanced, it was said, replaced, it was said, by some new downstream hatchery program. Well, that's not really a balanced exchange, not *quid pro quo*. Habitat has its limitations. We can supplement a little here and there, yes. But we can't cut a living river in half, and expect the bottom half to double. No matter how many hatcheries you build, how many fish you dump, the bottom half of a river doesn't double. There's a limit to how many fish a given stretch of river can sustain. That's just a simple fact. The truth is, the upper sections of most Pacific rivers, the sections that get dammed off, are, or were, the most productive parts of the systems for spawning, with lower water acidity and more food.

Maybe with turkeys it's more simple. They came out of Texas in boxes, from the hills of the Rio Grande. They look happy here, strut around Knox's horse pasture like proprietors, squat down in the grass like lazy cattle. I watched a flock of them, forty or so, peck along the riverbank up by Agnes one evening, myself on the Cougar

Lane Restaurant deck with a hamburger. There were plenty of happy clucks and yelps to go around.

Springtime gives that message. Even the problem fry in tank D, now that we've netted out a few that bloated up with stomach fungus, look happy and healthy.

Springtime soothes my misgivings as I circle the fry tanks, feeding the fish. Bird song and blue skies fill the valley. Back at our North Bank cabin springtime echoes with heron-clack from the rookery nestlings. The swallows grow bolder over the stoop, the wild azaleas grow sweeter. Deer wander everywhere. Raccoons scavenge everywhere. Butterflies drift everywhere. Black and yellow "army worms" crawl everywhere, creeping over the landscape, timid and relentless, all of those legs somehow perfectly controlled as they explore every crook and nook. The black widow spiders in the garage look shiny and fat.

The Curry Anadromous Fishermen all talk spring salmon. Wiry Clay F. wins the first-of-the-season contest prize with a ten-pounder, too small for a winner, some jokingly claim. Clay responds in good humor, says now that barbless hooks are part of the regulations above tidewater, the worms he uses for sturgeon fishing keep crawling off the hook.

May is no time for the fly-fisher around these parts, until late May, that is, when trout season opens, and you can roust through brush country after those hard-to-reach cutthroats. So I take an invitation from Dave Harris to go survey diving with him, in some local streams, to check out the populations of juvenile salmon and steelhead. "I'll find you a dry suit," he promises. "And a hood."

We meet at Indian Creek Hatchery at noon. We look over the fry and weigh them. In a couple weeks the coding wagon will be along to shoot their noses full of coded wire. We'll have to fast them first, starve them down to reduce stress, an odd but evidently valid procedure.

Dave and I dress at the hatchery for the dive, then hop in Dave's ODFW truck, and head up to Quosatana Creek, a feeder creek of the Rogue. It's not often you can get one of these fish biology guys captive, so I throw him a barrage of questions as we drive, get back a barrage of good answers. One thing I particularly note: he assures me that the Indian Creek fingerlings will not get released into the Rogue estuary until late August or September, a time of very low wild stock use. "Their impact on other stock should be pretty low, almost nil," he believes, and I am comforted. I can sow fish food with clearer conscience.

Dave has waterproof plastic writing slates and underwater markers, one for each pool, with bedrock and logs already sketched in from previous dives. We waddle upstream a couple hundred yards, float the first high pool, then a second. I've too much air in the dry suit and roll around on the surface, finding it hard to put down my feet.

"You look like a blueberry," Dave says, and shows me how to squat down, pull open the neck gasket, and squeeze out some air.

While I fiddle with gaskets, Dave's concerns are for the absence of fish in the pools; he's found nothing but one bunch of sticklebacks. He shakes his head. In the third pool, against a far rock wall where a log has fallen, lies a pocket filled with small steelhead and orangey yearling coho, a white slash on both the dorsal and anal fin of the coho as distinguishing marks. Dave is pointing this all out to me, chasing fish upstream to me, setting me up in the spots to watch them, all the while counting and marking on his slate. I try to stay upstream of him so as not to interfere too much with the census taking.

I'm impressed by the careful way Dave crisscrosses a pool, then stays a long time in the shallows, his head still underwater and canted to one side or the other, scanning the shorelines. He doesn't miss much, has a good eye, finds even the tiny steelhead hiding under rocks along the inch-water edges of Quosatana. But it sums to a disappointing count, all in all, with not a single sighting of juvenile chinook.

"Maybe we missed them," he says. "Maybe they got out ahead of us, or are still upstream. I hope so. But the carcass counts this winter were very low."

We go back to the truck and drive down to Lobster Creek. We dive the bridge pool. Underwater cable and wire are there along the bottom, nasty-looking stuff. Dave tells me it's the remains of washed-out gabions, evidence of how hard it is to build lasting enhancement structures in a stream this size. He swims across the stream into some rocks, and, through his snorkel, says, "Aha," or something like it, muffled and hollow, then pops up, and calls me over to see a big native cutthroat.

It's gone when I get there.

"About twenty inches," he says, above water this time, so that his words are clear. He holds apart his hands to show the size.

Dave moves on downstream and I stay above, my head in a cranny, looking down through a split of rock at young steelhead, my body shivering a little in the cold meltwater, the dry suit gasket squeezing my Adam's apple, my jaws clamped tight to hold off the chatter. When I rub on a rock, the cloud of particles I raise brings the small steelhead spurting around me, checking for morsels. They take things tentatively in their mouths, chew on them a little, then swallow or spit, as seems appropriate. The steelhead are of many sizes. On down further I find some more orange coho in a pocket under a fallen tree, and finally, down in the shallows below the bridge, Dave points out some silver-sided, green-backed juvenile chinook, four or five of them, about three inches long. One big sculpin holds on the bottom gravel surrounded by umbery salamanders in various coiled and wraparound postures of mating.

Tom Loynes, an ODFW staffer, shows up and gives his diving report from Jim Hunt Creek and Bark Shanty Hole upstream on Lobster Creek. He's seen good numbers of steelhead and coho, a couple of big native cutthroat, and a smattering of juvenile chinook. The chinook numbers in general are down, it seems, in Lobster, Quosatana, and Jim Hunt creeks. Dave gathers up the plastic slates. I ask if he's ever lost a slate, left it on a beach somewhere, and he says he hasn't. He will take the slates back to the office and enter the counts into a computer. He grins, and says again, "No, I never did lose one."

I pick a little miner's lettuce and offer it around. The stuff grows thick, is crisp and tasty. While I chew, the things I have learned this day banner across my mind. I have seen the steelhead all spread out in sizes, in multiple gradations, cycles overlapping in a complexity of sequence no hatchery can match. I have seen the oxygen bubbles spurting happily around, no need for dissolved-oxygen meters here. I have shivered in clean cold water, plenty cold enough, and plentiful in supply, as reliable as weather. I have watched the steelhead feed, all that easy food washing down to them steadily and naturally, no volunteers needed for six trips a day to the fry tanks and raceways. I have seen the clean creek bottoms, no brush and vacuum needed to clean away the grunge. I have seen the chosen nooks and eddies, the rock cover, the fallen-tree cover, the shade and dappling light, the varying currents—all those intricate and varied options there for wild fish to choose or reject. In short, it's homey water, sweet and sustaining. The conclusion seems obvious enough: a lot of our future efforts as STEP volunteers should go toward stream enhancement—reforesting the logged-off upper reaches of Lobster Creek, Quosatana Creek, and the myriad other creeks tumbling down to the Rogue, building some sturdier gabions to catch gravel for spawning, clearing away stream blockages to open up new miles of spawning areas, and, of course, protecting what prime spawning streams remain.

More Wednesdays pass, and the turkey hens disappear, no glimpse of them anywhere. A few morose jakes wander through the horse meadow. Then the hens reappear with chicks behind them in the grass, tiny speckled chicks bobbing and scurrying.

Meanwhile, in the tanks, the fry keep growing, feeding more boldly, swimming more strongly. One Wednesday I arrive and the majority of the salmon have been moved into a raceway, screened off from the intake and outlet, and allowed to stretch their fins. Fry tank D has the last of the hatchling fry, a problem lot.

For awhile they would not feed, and there were heavy morts, some of these sent up to the Fish & Wildlife labs for analysis. The report came back: starvation. There was one obvious variable from the three more successful tanks, A, B, and C—tank D was the only one not well shaded by a nearby myrtlewood. I threw some gunny sacks over the tank screen to give the fry some shade, shelter, and general peace-of-mind. It seemed to help a little, but they are still laggards, and bad feeders.

In the raceway, though, the salmon look active, healthy, mindlessly voracious, enormously swift and strong for their sizes, fusiform and fat. They take after their wild mothers, their wild fathers, green backs translucent in the morning glow, thick-bodied, burst-speeding beauties, a million years of survival wisdom in their genes.

Maybe we have it in our own genes, too—survival wisdom. I hope so. I hope we do better than the exhausted hummingbird in the hatchery shed. I hope we listen deep into ourselves, deep down into the land-rooted, water-rooted wisdom of our origins, and find our right way forward.

I wish that future for everyone and everywhere, but most particularly for the neighbors and myself of North Bank country, and for these rivers running close by our doorsteps.

∼

Riverbed

The buck in the yard this morning had antler velvet hanging down both sides of his face, hanging over both eyes, swinging as he walked. I glassed him just to make sure it was horn velvet. That's what it was, on a little two-point with gray streaks in his coat.

He'll be ready for rut, apple-sweet and randy. He's been joypopping those big King apples out back. At the moment, though, he looks a little comical, looks a little English-my-lord with a velvety wig.

The apple leaves are blanching vaguely yellow. The wooly-worms are marching across the highways in astonishing numbers. Out by the mailbox this morning I saw a marching wooly-worm no longer than a sow bug, some youngster, or some pygmy variety, and it seemed terribly vulnerable out there on the northbound-lane asphalt.

A few weeks back, sitting over sweet coffee on the stoop, I said to Catharine, "Something's changing. It smells like fall."

"You're right, " she said. "But what exactly is it that smells like fall?"

"Something the bears smell," I answered, and she gave me her indulgent smile.

Like the bears, I smell something in the air, something vague and punky, and think autumn thoughts of fishing. I find myself driven to a frenzy of fly tying and leader tying. This year's first idea—a Golden Hilton to match the famous Silver Hilton, but this one looking considerably like a jazzed-up Red Ant. I'm not sure just where the idea came from, probably just blew down the valley, up over the Snag Patch, and I lifted my nose into the fall-smelling breezes, moved my head ponderously back and forth, and found what I sniffed for, essence of Golden Hilton mixed right in there, mixed in with the smells of blackberry and deer dung, sly and savory.

House-fixing chores provoke an equal frenzy in me. I'm way behind the herons who finished up last spring, and I have the big cherry stump out front yet to do, as well, where it sits almost on top of the septic tank, a tricky dig ahead of me there, one sure to collide with a pipe or two, at the least.

But I have gotten the main bedroom finished, and gotten a local handyman, Mel P., and his son-in-law, out to sand and refinish the fir flooring. Mel underbid the job by considerable, not realizing how much gunk soaks up into fir, all his experience in oak. I paid him some extra. I reglued the bedroom ceiling where it had sagged and stained, sealed it and painted it, then under-papered the walls, watched the wet wrinkles dry to smooth, and papered that with a flowered pattern, though I put a hole through the paper on one top ceiling corner where I tried to get the moulding angles flush. The hole only barely shows, covered by the moulding. I left it, knowing how I would look at it everyday for six months and finally forget it. I got the lower walls wainscotted with western cedar left in the garage by the former owner and stacked in with a few dozen black widows and a couple thousand sow bugs, but a beautiful deep luster to the wood that I can find no match for at the local yards. The new thermalpanes in the three 4 x 5 windows look clear and clean, though I mismeasured one and had to scrap it and order a replacement pane, a wasteful mistake that undermined my measuring confidence for a few days and left me remeasuring everything, and then remeasuring again. I got foam insulation shot in around the framing, and new casements built, five coats of varnish over the stain, shades installed, mouldings up, doors sanded, stained, and varnished, closet rebuilt, baseboard heater rewired and repainted, and the pictures hung—three Charlie Russell prints that I salvaged from my father's study in Milwaukee and a Vermeer print in an antique Dutch frame of walnut, once cherished by my maternal grandparents. Though well-travelled, these pictures make a homey statement. They give the heraldic blood-stamp, and in matching colors, too.

A lot remained to do—several rooms and a back hallway needing floor work and ceiling work, the garage needing a new roof, the twelve apple trees scattered around the place badly needing pruning. Also the yard to mow, also four acres of log-rotting woodlands to brush out, also that bed to build, also that cherry stump to dig.

But to hell with it, I decided, one fall day; I needed a break, and headed up toward Lobster Creek, Golden Hiltons all new and bright in the fly box, freshly tied leaders all coiled and labeled in the leader pack.

I checked the Rogue's water level from various vantage points of the North Bank Road, and it looked high, the water a dam-release brown mixed with green "scudge." Two weeks previous the river had hardly flowed, water temperature in the seventies, gaunt banks yellow-green with dried duckweed clinging to rocks like shrunken rawhide. Now all that was changed and flowing, but the reports I'd heard on steelhead were not encouraging. The ODFW seinings at Huntley Creek had taken only a few small half-pounders.

I parked at the Lobster Creek Bridge, south side, and walked down through the old campground, down through the blackberries and the snake grass, waded a couple of side channels, and pushed out through brown roil of that first pour-off above the bridge. The river had changed. I'd fished it December, January, February, March, April and not seen the changes, but this time, now that the water had dropped, I saw the changes—a whole new slick on the south side, before me, the bottom part not so good, but the upper part much better than the previous year, gouged out by last-winter floods, its gravel tumbled down to new places. I fished it high and low, but caught nothing, and hiked across the bridge to the north side, climbed the long climb down the bank, waded out to the old gravel spit, a reliable spot the previous season, but the flow now changed, the lie gone. So I waded on down below the bridge, finding gravel bars where they had not been before, finding footing almost to the base of Massacre Rock.

Massacre Rock, massive and willow topped, stood solid amidst all this churning, shifting riverbed. It was named for the slaughter of Native Americans coming downriver in their canoes, the soldiers hiding behind this rock in ambush, and it is not the only named rock hereabouts, either. There's Elephant Rock down toward the mouth, *Samuel Roberts, 1850* carved on its face, and named rocks all up and down the coast. There's Pistol River Rock from which, it's said, the local natives took their name—Chetl-essentans, "people of the big rock." There's Kissing Rock just a mile south of town, and Black Rock, Cave Rock, Mack Arch, Yellow Rock, Leaning Rock, House Rock, and Rainbow Rock. There's Sister Rocks to the north, halfway to Port Orford, and Battle Rock right there on the Port Orford beach, and Tichenor Rock, Klooqueh Rock, and the whole Port Orford Reef made up of named rocks, Castle Rock on north of that, and a few hundred others. Then there are all those capes and headlands standing solid enough to hold names—Cape Ferrelo that we drive over to get to Brookings, Cape Sebastian where we go to hike and watch for whales, Cape Blanco, where the land juts out further west than anywhere else in Oregon, and where the wind always blows the hardest.

The world is full enough of named rocks, I thought, standing there up to my knees in Rogue current. I remembered Saint Brigid's altar, near the old parish church of Killinagh, a deep cavity worn into rock by a turning river stone. You turn the stone inside the rock hole and curse your enemies as the stone turns. Done rightly, it's said, the curse takes. There's the Blarney Stone, too, and the Lia Fail, Stone of Destiny, reputed to roar under the rightful king of old Ireland. The Irish like their stones, the way they like their brew, because, I would guess, a stone stays put, tells no lies, does not drive you off home ground to the western barrens for your faith, and, moreover, says nothing when you get there.

Think of them all: the Black Stone of Mecca; gravestones; boundary stones; naval stones; meteorites in gold, worn as charms by the old Greeks; Stonehenge, Chaco Canyon, and the Medicine Wheel. Up on the hilltop we see to the northeast of the North Bank cabin there are ancient circles of piled stone—"spirit rings" the locals call them.

Some years ago, up in the Yukon, I hauled my family out of the way some miles to find a boulder at the head of Teslin Lake. We stopped at various outposts to get directions, then found the boulder where it lay, and witnessed the imbedded footprints of the Raven Father. Local myth tells that this boulder was the Raven's last perch after he created the world, everything still pretty hot and molten then, and blistery on the Raven Father's toes. Were a white man like myself to climb up and put feet to the imprints, the skies would cloud over and rain commence—so says the myth. The same myth holds that if the natives ever run out of fish, they need only tie an inflated fish bladder to this boulder and roll it into the Yukon River.

We could use a boulder like that along the Rogue. We could use a boulder like that for the whole coastal fishery.

I caught nothing above Lobster Creek Bridge that day except a whiff of change, the shiftings of pebbles, and nothing the next morning up at Coal Riffle, either, except the recollection that Coal got its name when a boat load of coal, mined upriver, capsized there. And I wondered just where in the riverbed that coal was now, how many miles downstream it had crept and bottomed in the ninety-odd years since, or how long it had taken to crumble.

Coal riffle had changed, too, since the previous summer, the bottom washout shallower on roadside, the deeper channel curving more to the far side now, farther out than formerly, harder to reach for the roadside fly-caster. These lower-river gravel bars have an easy wading, free-casting charm to them, but they take some seasonal figuring.

The old gent just parking ahead of my car on the high bank above Coal one morning had seen some river changes. He opened up the back end of his truck, said "Stay" to the Brittany female in the portable kennel there, started fitting together his worming gear, and said to me, "Oh, gosh. The river hasn't changed much this year. Not like it used to. Not like when we had some floods."

We chatted about fishing, discussed the Klamath, the Trinity, the Sacramento, the Rogue. He'd fished them all, and seen their runs deteriorate. "The dam just did it for the Rogue and all that," he said. "Not to offend you, but that Corps of Engineers, now, they just don't know nothin' about rivers, how they work. All they know is how to build dams. It used to be we had caddis on this river, and stone flies. God did we have the stone flies! I haven't seen them like they used to be for years. They started disappearing, along with the fish, just after they put in that Lost Creek Dam up there by Prospect. You can't mess around with the food chain. Willow and alder growing out on the gravel bars, now, messing up the spawning. I tell you."

He shook his head at my luck, commiserating. "You didn't do so good down there, huh? Well, it's a little late in the morning for flies."

I unlaced my boots, pulled off my leaky waders, changed socks.

"Oh I still get a few on worms," he allowed. "I got nineteen one morning up above here, some pretty good ones, too, seven, eight pounds. You have to find the channels."

"The channels that move," I said.

The next day I fished Fry's Landing, the channel I used to wade across to the island all but gone, just a trickle. I ran a Juicy Bug carefully from top to bottom down the main channel without a touch, then found, at the island's base, a deep channel against the island's bank that had never been there at all the previous year.

Up on the North Umpqua, The Station changed periodically, that first slick below the confluence of Steamboat Creek and the main river. Some years it hollowed out and held lots of steelhead. Other years it filled in and wasn't productive. The wade out to it, from the south bank, never changed much, though, always an up-and-down affair across the same bedrock holes and ledges worn smooth by many crossings. All those boulders, ledges, cliffs of the North Umpqua hold their places through winter, like Massacre Rock and Elephant Rock on the Rogue, and not much gravel moves in the river to reshape the bottom, only the occasional log inconveniently jammed in some slot. It's a very reassuring stretch of river, the fly water of the North Umpqua, constant and predictable, a bedrock river.

Upriver on the Rogue, of course, it, too, struts its bedrock—up in Huggins Canyon, Mule Creek Canyon, Kelsey Canyon, all deep and tumbling, and down lower yet, in Copper Canyon, and along those river ledges just above Agnes, places I favor, never much changed from season to season.

The other evening I drove upriver to fish the dog watch, and found Jack, an August regular, upstream of me at Coal, at the top part of the run. He's an elder man, not much of a caster, but he knows the places. "There's a little place washed out up here this year," he said, "where I've picked up a few."

The previous year he'd told me how good it used to be up above the riffle, until the dredging operation on the far side of the river, for the jetboat channel, pushed all the gravel over onto the south side, pretty much ruining the slick for south-side fishing. "I used to go up there, catch a bunch, come back down and catch a bunch, then go back up above and catch some more. I'd just keep going back and forth like that from four to seven every evening."

We sat on a weathered drift board laid across rocks, and compared wading shoes, and compared reels, his an old Pfleuger, still turning, and compared lack of success on the evening. "How'd you do last year after I left?" he asked. "Did more fish come up?"

I told him they had, some good fish.

"Maybe this year too, then. Maybe they're just late. There sure aren't very many here. I've been here ten days and caught twelve fish, most of them small."

We watched a salmon jump. "I've been fishing some down at the bend," I told him. "At Fry's Landing."

"Doing any good?"

"No. Less pressure, though, nobody there but myself, in fact."

"I used to fish Big Fish Riffle a lot. I don't anymore. It's pretty much all filled in with gravel. Fish go over it, of course, but they don't stay. That's the next one down below Fry's, you know."

I said I knew. We went back out in the river and fished.

Gravel moved under my feet in the current. I remembered star garnets, big as golf balls, I'd dug out of Emerald Creek up in Idaho. I remembered those Sweetwater agates we used to find, tumbled and round, in the dry riverbeds of Wyoming, all of them weathered out of some hill or dale, rolling slowly across the earth. I remembered that piece of slate I'd picked off a gravel bar on the Klamath River, fishing down there one Thanksgiving, near Dutch Creek, three holes drilled in the slab, stone-drill work in-slanted from both sides, red dye still blazing across its bottom—a gorget, Native American ceremonial neck piece. Some seasonal swerve of the Klamath must have cut a Shasta or Pit River grave, taken a bank of the river and moved it on downstream, and the gorget with it.

Rivers do things like that, keep changing the channels, making new beds, stripping those gravel sheets, washing old places clean, then making the beds up again for summertime, taut and cornered and new, with a few surprises under the pillow, some tooth fairy drop, some blind hole for the unwary wader to step into. I recalled how the Snag Patch channel used to be the main channel of the Rogue before the main channel moved on over to the south side. It used to be that the faded duplex beyond Neighbor S.'s place was a riverbank motel.

Even the home landscape turns strange in the effusion of spring and its effect. It's all standard practice, though, inland sea change, the usual high water chores of winter, pushing and rolling, scooping and grinding, twisting and shifting down to the juggernaut tides. The river gods don't want us waders and casters taking things for granted, feeling too confident, feeling too secure in our head-maps of river bottom. They don't want those spawning beds left untossed, and unscoured, either. Permanence of place proves a shifty concept in this season, but under its wandering foil of gravel the bedrock stands, and if I stay long enough in these parts, I expect to see the patterns of riverbed repeat themselves, gravel covering and then uncovering the bedrock base in varying years.

Just some days ago Catharine and I climbed that hill northeast of the cabin to see if we couldn't find one of those fabled "spirit rings." We climbed clear to the top of the hill where the Douglas fir are so windswept and rock rooted that they look dwarfed and stunted with tossed-about tops like coastal cypress. Up there on top you can find places where a vista of the Rogue spreads out below you to the south, the Pacific spreads out to the west, and you feel pretty high-up in the world. At the same moment you can still hear the surf pounding, and see the white of it down at the Rogue's mouth past the Wedderburn bridge.

We looked around all over that rocky hilltop, splitting up finally. I walked north until the trees densed up too much, then came back and whistled. Catharine shouted back that she'd found one. What she showed me, when I went her way, a smile flickering along the edges of her lips, was a cement cistern dug in by some developer or other for a building lot.

"You mean that's not one?" she said.

"Well it's round," I said.

On the way back down we found our spirit ring, piled four or five boulders high, and big enough for a person to lie down in, which made me wonder if the ring wasn't an ancient wind shelter of some sort. There are primitive circle shelters like that still standing over in the upper Rogue Valley, certain places, up on the slopes of Roxy Ann for instance. This one we'd found had a hefty myrtlewood growing up through the center of it, and tied on one myrtlewood limb was a neon-yellow survey ribbon, marking the spirit of the times, I suppose.

From where we stood I could look down and see Elephant Rock, and it struck me, suddenly, that the gravel beach above the dark, tree-covered hump of the rock, and the visible slick running down in front of the rock, must be that place I'd heard mentioned once or twice, a good place for fly-fishing. That slick was only one bend down from Johns Hole, but a place I'd never fished, and never knew was so close to our cabin.

Riverbed

Whoever had sat that spirit ring, with the salmon-bulging Rogue stretched down there below, must have known this Rogue landscape, and must have known Elephant Rock, though certainly by some other name. And standing there beside that circle of spirit rocks, I had my own inspiration. I'd haul my kayak over to the Snag Patch the very next chance I got, then float on down below, around the bend, with my fly rod along, and see just what I could find down there at bedrock-solid Elephant Rock that had gone exactly nowhere in a good many years.

~

Smolts

The ODFW wire-coding wagon showed up this morning at Indian Creek Hatchery. When I got there at eight, Ron Lukas, the hatchery volunteer manager, was bent over Raceway Two while an ODFW biologist from Portland, Bill Haugen, was hooking up the intake and outflow hoses to the truck. Three local women sat inside the truck on stools handling the wire-coding machines.

Ron and I ran a divider screen down Raceway One, herding the parr into a greater concentration, to make the netting easier.

"Come on, let me show you the coding stuff," Ron offered, and led me up into the truck's interior, introduced me to the women—Berma, Donna, Mary Ann—and showed me how the rig operated. The netted parr went first into a bath of anesthetic. When the parr keeled over onto their sides, they went into a tray of fresh water from which the women dipped them out, one by one.

"You can do a few if you want," said Donna, and moved aside for me. I dipped out a parr, small and slippery in my hand, but inert, turned it upside down, clipped off the rubbery adipose fin close to the back with a scissors to signal hatchery origins, then tried clumsily to press the snout to the apparatus that shot coded wire.

"Squeeze it a little," Donna said, "so its mouth opens. Then put the mouth over that little knob on the mold. That positions it. Now hit the button."

There was a round gray button the size of a half-dollar at the machine's bottom. I pushed it. The machine shuddered. I couldn't tell if anything had happened.

"Well, toss it into the return pipe and we'll see," Donna said.

The return pipe had a stop-door activated by a wire sensor. If you missed getting a wire into a parr's snout, the door didn't open, and the parr got re-routed, dropping back into a bucket of water under the sink near your feet. My parr came this route. I sloshed around with one hand in the bucket, got the parr, squeezed it again, put its snout to the anvil again, pushed the button. Something must have gone into the snout this time because the stop-door opened for the little salmon and it slid down the long return hose into Raceway Two, fluttered down through the water like a finished skipping stone, and lay there on its side on the bottom looking dead.

"That one'll have its fins under it again in a couple of minutes," said Bill. "So to speak."

"How many you lose in this process?" I asked, thinking they must lose a lot. But no, Bill said; there's less loss with wire-coding than with fin-clipping. "Probably about twenty morts on the day, and we'll be doing about ten thousand."

"You do this every day?"

"Never know where I'll be from one day to the next. We do the coast, the Columbia, the Deschutes." His hand waved across an imaginary landscape. "Get orders and we move on to the next place."

I smiled a little at the grand sweep of his description. "It's a good system," he added. "Seriously. We learn a lot from the codes, a lot more than we could from fin-clips. This wire, for example, reads 7-51-29. That tells us both the date and the fact that these are Indian Creek fish."

I needed no convincing. A commercial fisher up in Washington catches a salmon, sees the adipose clip, saves the head. The snout gets frozen, sent to a fisheries laboratory in Clackamas, Oregon, and a researcher there punches one more coordinate into the computer files. Fisheries students get hired to check various ocean catches for wire-tags. Biologists gather snouts from dead and spawned-out salmon in various streams. Anglers turn in heads from fin-clipped catches. In a good year, ODFW might get back seventy thousand wire-tags out of some seven million tagged smolts, roughly one in one hundred. The statistics add up and up. Pretty soon the biologists might know, for example, that planting B in the Rogue River is showing up heavily in commercial catches, while planting A is not, and the causes of that disparity get attention.

The river cycles of these fish are pretty well documented and understood. Wire-coding helps fill in some vitally needed ocean information. That hatchery fish lend themselves so readily to wire-coding and consequent ocean research is one strong reason to raise them.

I went off to get the dissolved-oxygen meter, and took some readings, everything looking normal. There would be no feeding today because of the coding, an unexpected respite for me, a free Wednesday, and the weather balmy. More projects waited at the North Bank cabin, as always, but they could wait. I had a place I wanted to go.

There are still native cutthroat in this country, back in the deep hills, back in the cougar canyons where the coastal rivers start. So I'd heard, here and there, no one speaking of it too loudly.

I had my own ideas of where to go, had asked Tim Unterwegner, local head of ODFW, about one place I had in mind, and he'd looked up, a little startled. "Well, yes," he'd allowed. "There are, in fact, some cutthroat up there. I've never been back there myself." He'd had that quality about him that I remembered from Yellowstone National Park days, trying to get a permit for the backcountry, a permit for places where the park rangers really didn't want anybody to go.

"Just catch-and-release?" he'd asked.

When I'd nodded affirmative, he'd thawed a little. "I heard it's beautiful back in there. The Forest Service did a fish survey in that country some years back. I talked to the guy who did it."

So I drove, Wednesday, kayak on the roof rack, and reached put-in about noon, then kayaked upstream another couple of miles, crossed the river from roadside, the road high and above, almost beyond hearing, hid the kayak one place, the paddle another, pulled on my waders and wading boots, and headed up the feeder stream to see what I could find.

The pools held deep and clear, with more caddis along the bottom than I had thought to find. Frogs leaped out from the banksides every few yards. It was nice to see some frogs again, always a good sign. No roads, no paths, no beer bottles, no snarls of monofilament, no fire rings, no footprints but those of deer and coon, and the canyon steepened up within a mile of the mouth. I kept on, crossing back and forth through the stream, from gravel bar to gravel bar, the crossings all deeper than they looked, waist-deep sometimes even at the pool run-outs.

The cliff sides weren't sheer, but slanted. A gray serpentine formed the base, with a reddish clay higher, great knobs of roots curling out over space here and there where a pin oak or pine had found some room to grow. But the cliffs were high and scrabbly, no way that I could see to get up them, or down them. Gravel plateaus from high water years spread out sometimes along the creek with deer paths across them. Once I found an east-facing knoll and climbed it, checking around for obsidian chippings without success. But mostly it was narrow canyon with a pool every quarter mile or so, clean greenish pools that tempted me to jump in and go swimming.

I followed the stream on up several miles before I tied on a big grasshopper imitation and dapped it around on a pool. I thought I'd probably gotten above most of the steelhead juveniles, but no. Every other cast they sucked at the hopper, or bumped it around in circles, occasionally hooking themselves. I was careful with them. I always thought I was careful with smolts, but now that I've worked with them, know what time and feeding goes into the growth of each one, I am more careful yet. Despite that care, one hooked itself in the eye. The hook was barbless and came out easily. I held the smolt in my hand a long time in the current. It swam off vigorously enough, but the eye is a bad place; the eye and the tongue and the gills—all bad places to hook fish, if you want them to survive a release. So I tied on a number eighteen caddis, fished with it on up, thinking it would be too small to do much damage to the juveniles, kept catching them, despite trying not to, and another one somehow hooked itself in the eye.

They're ferocious, that's the reason. Most of them strike three times as hard as a cutthroat, literally hurling themselves at a fly, over it, past it. I suppose, with attacks like that, it's inevitable that sooner or later one hooks itself in the eye.

I stopped fishing, hiked on up higher, another mile or so. Typically the cutthroat stay above the juvenile salmon and steelhead, way up in the headwaters. I guess I never got high enough. When I tried fishing again, there were more smolt, so I stopped fishing altogether, just sat down and enjoyed the place, the ouzels and the solitude.

That was the day, shooting wire up juvenile snouts in the morning, putting metal through their eyes in the afternoon. Somehow it seemed like a nice day anyhow, though a thinking one, wondering how to fish these waters without being destructive, wondering whether to come back in the fall for adult steelhead, or to leave this place alone, as sanctuary. Maybe the latter. Maybe just leave it alone, come up here with Catharine sometime for a swim and a hike, bring a diving mask, leave the fishing gear at home. Anyway, it was nice to know that it was here, a hidden and untouched place.

Going back down the canyon I stumbled and fell into some rocks, bruised up my leg, and lay there for a minute. Silver flashed in the sun just below me. I hauled myself upright, and waded down. Dead in the shallows lay a spring chinook, fresh and bright and firm, but, yes, very dead. I had heard reports that down in the main river chinook had been catching a gill disease from the unseasonably warm and low water. This one at my feet had never spawned, showed no kipe, and no darkening. It was, in fact, in considerably better shape than a lot of salmon I'd seen kept by anglers. But I left it there, twenty-odd pounds of dining for the buzzards, and went on home.

A few days later I tried again for native cutthroat, this time further south on a different river, way up high where the access road turns gravel, veers northerly, and the river dwindles down to a fern-sided creek. Smolt rose everywhere there, too, with golden bellies, some of them. I kept going higher, then still higher, catching a cutthroat here and there, but also smolt.

The cuts ran small, eight inches and less, all head and not a pretty fish proportionally, though the markings pretty, so many spots on them that, coming to the fly, they looked black. Nobody ever said these coastal rivers were food rich. That's one reason why the Klamath and the Columbia are such major producers of steelhead. Those rivers cut the Coast and Cascade ranges and claim a whole eastern side where the acidity of the water is less and the feed more.

"Hell yes," said Tim Unterwegner, explaining this to me. "There are ten times more juveniles in the Deschutes than you'll find in these coastal rivers. It's the pH mostly."

These coastal cutthroat looked two years old, maybe three, by the heads, then tapered back to the tails like a carrot, and looked yearling or younger in the body. They rose prettily to a dry fly, though, and jumped sometimes.

Way up above a last faint feeder creek, I found a couple of good pools, a few cuts, several paths down through the ferns where some locals knew their ways, but even there I found steelhead smolts, and set back too hard on a strike, jerking the smolt high. It flew through the air and came down smack on a rock. I worked on that smolt for fifteen minutes. It never stopped swimming in circles.

So I quit fishing, walked on down the river toward where I'd parked the car, and crossed beside a deadwater pool, isolated from the river by a long gravel bar, some twenty small steelhead trapped there by drought and falling water. I went down on my knees with my hat. Eight fingerlings I managed to catch in a half-hour of scrambling, carrying each one carefully back to the river in my hat, watching each one swim away into the mother current.

That was good fishing—hat-dipping, mud-kneeling fishing of the first order; and good for the conscience, good for the mind, a payback of sorts for those brained and blinded victims of my sport. The small bodies of those fingerlings wiggled with gladness (I think it was gladness), as they swam free of their puddle prison, free of my hat, and back into the river race, with no wire in them, anywhere.

～

The Blue Closet

In the North Bank study sits a honeysuckle woodbine soap jar holding three white ostrich plumes. The strands of them wave gently in the room's cross-breeze. Yesterday in the yard I picked up a blue heron feather, soft and hackle perfect. Last December, at the National Car Rental counter of the Grand Junction airport, I reached into my jacket pocket for some money, and brought forth a handful of flicker feathers, black and golden tail feathers picked off a back ridge of Geisel Hill. I'd thought they might make good dry fly wings.

Rainy winter nights on the North Bank, with a myrtle-wind rustling along the eaves, the woodstove stoked, hot tea in my brownstone mug, I open the blue closet and get out the old Nottingham cigar boxes where I store my fly tying materials. I poke through the fading skins of starling and pheasant, the golden capes of exotica, the strips of moose hide and elk gathered from various Montana taxidermists, the salted hides of duck and quail and grouse from various lowland and upland hunts out of the past, these last packaged in plastic bags, and I set up the tying vice, turning the setscrew gently until the vice holds firm on the middle oak plank of the kitchen table.

Something wistful and recollective emanates from the materials and the screw-turn of the vice, but also something immediate and needful. This fly tying has been a home process, or an attempt at home process, in seven states and ten cities that come to mind offhand. The feathers and furs themselves layer in their boxes like sediment laid down in different ages. If I dig down deep enough in a larger box I keep, I can still find a rabbit-fur collar ripped off a rummage-sale coat when I was not yet a teenager, and dyed feathers from women's hats of the same era. Long ago these should have moldered and mildewed in the natural processes of the world, or dropped shredded to earth in coyote scat or owl pellet, and composted back down into the turning cycles of rabbits and birds, but a few judicious mothballs, a dry box, a deep layering in dark closets, and they have survived.

The need that rouses me to tying, beyond recollection and an urge for home-form, mostly concerns the next day's fishing. The sporting shops sell workable flies, of course, but not my flies, not the proportion nor the color nor the weight I favor. If the weight is there in those shop flies, then it is probably noxious lead-wire weight in the underwrapping, and every lost fly becomes another dollop of poison in a river.

Then, too, there aren't many established fly patterns that I follow to the letter. Much of the pleasure of tying flies comes from creating new patterns from the materials available, and seeing how those patterns work on the fish. A personal style emerges, and a personal judgement of what looks good and what works well. Of course, these habits and tastes change over time, with the consequence that I can look at my flies and tell their period. They too, like the materials in their boxes, layer in time, depending on the whims and needs of each year and season.

The flies I have tied on and off now through four decades vary from state to state largely because the trout and insects have varied from state to state. But another cause of difference lies in the kinds of local materials that come to hand. In Wisconsin there were bluebills and muskrats to be had, in Montana elk hair and moose mane from the local taxidermists, in Bear Creek Valley of the upper Rogue plenty of pheasants and mountain quail. More recent acquisitions of mylars, nylons, and polypropylenes sprinkle over the surfaces of the Nottingham boxes. From all these materials comes the mix on the hook with the evening's thoughts, and what results is a personal pattern, or a series of patterns, different and unexpected, that mark home ground with small nativities.

Tying attractor flies for steelhead is not a match-the-hatch kind of proposition, generally, but a visual process, looking for combinations of color and form to ground a personal belief. Color, flash, and the big sizes once lured me, but now I believe more in olives, grays, and browns that give meaning to a modest touch of color. Now I believe in a little weight and a deeper-running fly, and in smaller sizes, and in motion, the allure of imitated life. Flutter and subtlety hold my current faith. They accord with the slow dance of the myrtlewood tops across the North Bank Road from the kitchen. These days a yellow-and-olive dubbed body of rabbit hair, a reddish wing of squirrel tail salvaged from a local road kill, and a wrap or two of grouse hackle, all on a number eight black salmon hook, make a fly that haloes itself with my gut and intuitive belief, and that belief keeps my feet a little warmer in the river currents of December. I asked Catharine to name this pattern on the night of its creation. She looked at the fly for a minute and said, "Looper Dooper."

For years sculpin patterns filled my fly boxes. I had an old sculpin pattern Frank Moore had tied, reputed his favorite fly on the North Umpqua. From it evolved my own pattern, tied with two fox hair wings, front and back on the hook, and flappy saddle-hackle wings. Because steelhead feed heavily on sculpin at sea, also in the estuaries, I thought this fly triggered latent feeding reflexes. It was a nice thought on a slow day. I fished unweighted sculpins sometimes, as dry flies, sometimes grease-lined them, sometimes quartered them, sometimes riffled them cross-stream. The fly worked for all seasons, on the Umpqua, a good many of those flies chewed to shreds before retirement. Naturally, then, I began with sculpins on the Rogue; but the longer I fished them on the Rogue the more my belief in them shrivelled, dried up, blew away in the williwaws off the Bear Camp summit, and did not return.

The first stumblebum Rogue season, as I cast to all the wrong places at all the wrong levels, the sculpin pattern became the focus of everything I did wrong, empty Rogue day following empty Rogue day, all my Umpqua hubris dashed and blinded.

It is a quirky and primitive thing that an adult and educated human being should encapsulate luck in a fishing fly. But I seem to have done that. And then undone that. My Umpqua skills, such as they were, shaded with derivation. I had learned from others most of the skills, and many of the best places. When my luck left me on the Rogue, sneaking off like the spirit of Hercules deserting Antony, I did not know at first just how to react or which way to turn.

Faced with empty Rogue days and a knowledge vacuum, I finally considered some changes. I scratched the Umpqua methods and started over. I looked hard at the water, and fished different places. I looked hard at water depth, and fished deeper. I looked hard at the sculpins, tied too large and too light for the Rogue anyway, and moved them from the fishing vest to that blue hallway closet.

I fished that fall with a sink-tip line and a weighted Street Walker variant tied with a black-purple body and just a hint of purple mylar under a modest hair wing. The fly pattern meant comparatively little to my improving results, of course, only the repository of everything else I was learning—the riffles, the ways to wade them, the sweet spots, the times to fish them, the depths to fish them.

But I haven't cast a Street Walker for over a year. There's the Looper Dooper now. Then, too, one day out in the yard of the North Bank cabin I started watching the herons. They fly almost constantly across our patch of sky, sometimes cutting behind the house, sometimes cutting north behind the pines, sometimes slanting right up between house and garage. I began the habit of sitting outside on balmy evenings and watching the herons in their endless feeding treks. One nest I could see from the driveway. When I glassed it, I found that the young were almost the size of adults. No wonder they took so much feeding, and late feeding too. The flights of the parents continued on into dusk and early dark, maybe longer. The squawks and shrieks went on all night.

I joked with my wife that the nests must be getting a little crowded up there in the pines, with so many growing bodies crammed together, so many sharp beaks on awkward youngsters. At three in the morning I sometimes jerked upright in bed as a resounding squawk echoed through the window screen, and smiled to myself at the thought of a pine-top goosing, rolled back down into the covers and kept listening. Neighbor H., however, says marauding coons cause those nighttime squawks.

None of the neighbors complains at all about this nocturnal chorus. I think they're rather proud of the herons. It would not surprise me if they also thought them lucky, like old-world cranes.

The herons didn't drop that many feathers, but I picked one or two out of the yard every week, and more at mowing time, for after herding the garter snakes out of the tall grass so that they wouldn't get chopped, and chasing the mower in circles past all the fringes of fern and holly, I covered more yard than I normally did in my searches, and the feathers were always there, tipped this way and that between the leaves and the fern stalks.

My stash of these feathers grew for some time before any use for them occurred to me. Then one evening I pulled them out under the kitchen light and considered them. I was running low on a pattern I call the Gray Panther, a pattern that began as a bucktail caddis streamer. After catching a couple of accidental steelhead on it one day on the Umpqua, I played with the pattern off and on, changed it from a true caddis orange to a deeper steelhead orange, added a gold tag, a gray butt and gray hackle.

On the North Bank, that evening under the kitchen light, I was fresh out of gray hackle. Those heron feathers were mostly gray, a blue-gray, though some of them were white and gray. I'd seen some patterns like the Sol Duc made of palmered heron. So I tried a Gray Panther with heron and was startled: those heron feathers were supple. They palmered with ease. The Gray Panther looked very handsome and buggy with a palmered heron over the brown-orange body, and a few strands of gold mylar under the wing for a touch of flash.

It's a home-place bonus of the North Bank that this ideal hackle, this old-world-lucky hackle, comes floating down to me from the local skies. In these days of protected species, heron hackle is actually an illegal commodity, so I am twice lucky to have my own harmless and private supply.

One slow evening, up above Agnes, having fished my fill with assorted other flies, I pulled out an ugly, gray-black nymph, tied it on, and promptly hooked two steelhead. Maybe that was happenstance, but you never know, so I went home and tied up some variants using goose primary for the split tail, flattening the wrappings of brass wire with a pliers, braiding a mylar thread through a purple-black body, and hackling the thorax with gray heron. The finished fly glittered a little but not too much, looked bug ugly, and had my immediate belief.

That was the birth of the Heron Nymph, bathed in a halo of Rogue moonlight through the skylight shafts. I pushed back from the tying vice and toasted the new creation with a slug of cold tea from the almost forgotten mug. I knew I had a home-place, North Bank pattern.

Today I telephoned Neighbor H., who owns the pines of the heron rookery, the base, as it were, and introduced myself. He's a volunteer fellow feeder of the Indian Creek Hatchery juvenile chinook, Sunday his day. So we had a common interest. I asked him if I could come up and look for feathers under the rookery itself.

"Come on up!" he said.

We hiked around through the whitewashed ferns, sidestepped two fallen and rotting young heron, picked up pieces of blue-green shell and a few feathers, not as many as I had hoped. Neighbor H. leaned over below me and picked a chinook fry out of the ferns.

"Look at that," he said. "Still fresh. Not even stiff."

We looked it over, fingered it, sniffed it.

"I'll just throw it here for the coons," he said.

He took me on a tour of his place, showed me giant crickets inside his spring, showed me his "old growth" poison oak, fed me a sweet plum, some fresh raw peas, some raspberries, a hazelnut, dug me some potatoes for dinner, showed me a beehive cleverly housed inside an old refrigerator and cabled tightly to a tree to discourage the bears, and then his butcher's band saw and grinder inside the garage.

"You can use this anytime you want," he said of the butcher's saw. "Bear, deer, whatever."

I asked what he knew about the place we owned. He named a few names, then laughed. "Tell you what I remember," he said, "was the time my dad blew a stump on the hillside there. Used a little too much dynamite. A part of the root flew clear across the creek and landed over on your roof. We got a phone call from those folks real quick. I'm telling you, that was a long ways for a hunk of wood to jump."

I came home with those potatoes in a bag, pea pods in my pants pockets, a new feeling of neighborhood in my head, and a bunch of heron hackle in my hat.

I figure it this way. Herons hassled steelhead smolts all down their long river voyage to the sea. So I'll play on those memories, harness those lingering steelhead resentments, and offer them a bit of heron on a hook. I'll carry a fly box full of heron nymphs around with me, canyon to canyon, stone to stone, like a talisman.

~

I've got some old flies all sorted out by patterns in the compartments of two equally old Wheatly fly boxes and stacked on a shelf in the blue closet. My father bought those flies, already in the Wheatly boxes, from a gentleman in Rice Lake, Wisconsin, that same fellow who sold him the Granger split-bamboo rod, back in the thirties. I used to use some of the caddis flies on brown trout in a creek just outside of Eau Claire, Wisconsin. I'd park at the bridge, shag over a couple of pine-crested hills, and come out in a dry-grass meadow with the trout rising there every summer evening. I lost a lot of those caddis flies on that stretch, but it didn't seem to matter, there being so many of them and all. Before long, however, certainly before any alarm went off in my brain, the caddis pattern vanished from the Wheatly compartments.

Lots of other dry patterns remain in the Wheatly boxes, though, all tied on squarish hooks, the bends almost right-angled; lots of double upright wings with dun bodies, quill bodies, colors not of the standard, whether different colored or faded is hard to tell; lots of partridge hackle on coffee-brown dubbing, with white upright wings, or lead upright wings; a few Parmachene Belles and Gordons; but mostly dark flies. Whoever tied these flies favored the sultry and shadowy hues, and favored heavy dressing—thick hackle, double wings, all beautifully tied, tight and tidy, balanced and reserved.

I take these old flies out and look at them sometimes, pick one out here, one out there, hold it up to the light, wonder about it, put it back, and always think to find somebody who knows flies and ask about these. A couple weeks ago, hearing rumors of a fly-fishing museum up in Florence, Oregon, I made a phone call to the Florence operator, but she could find no listing of a fly-fishing museum. She did find a number for a fly shop in nearby Reedsport. I called there and left a message on the machine. The next day came a phone call back with news that such a museum existed in Florence, yes, the Cushner Museum, but the proprietor had just died, and the museum, presumably, was closed down. So I put that project on hold.

A few weeks ago I went over to a local garage sale to buy some brass screws and picked up, as well, an old fishing rod. It's a six-foot piece of bamboo wrapped with cord up the bottom third, the cord decoratively knotted around a primitive reel seat. The cord is brown with varnish and well worn. The three guides along the shaft look like miniature barrels about one-half inch long. This rod caught its share of fish in the hog lines at the Rogue's mouth, I was told, and I believe it. It's up on my study wall now where I can look at it and remember the hog lines and the way the salmon pushed in to the river's mouth.

I've a couple old fly reels, too, and have been thinking about the various reels I keep in the closet above the cat bed—two of the reels so lightweight they've fallen apart, another one with heavy disc brakes, and no pawl click. The two I really like are the old ones— my dad's antique Bakelite "Henshall No. 102" Weber, too small for steelhead, and my antique Hardy Perfect, cold-welded into some stability after a shattering fall on the Sacramento, but altogether too fragile at this point for steady use.

It's the older sounds I like, that make the difference, that prayer wheel of the pawl click. Sure the disc brake reels are smoother. Smoothness is not the point with me. What I need is a couple new reels with old sounds, old-fashioned pawl click sounds, and I'll make them into special North Bank reels, associate the sounds with seals, sea lions, beavers, and night herons at Johns Hole, and long screaming runs at the edges of darkness up at Coal Riffle.

Those new silent reels are no new idea, of course, and once were made that way for a good reason. Out on the chalk streams you can spook a trout by pulling out line from a clicking reel. Old-timers sometimes put the reel under a vest or coat to pull out line, muffling the sounds. But the Rogue is not the Beaverkill. I'm not worried about spooking steelhead with my reel. I like to hear a steelhead run, gauge its run by the pitch of the reel's scream, and like to listen to what a fish is doing, use my ears for that and use my eyes to get to shore from a deep wade.

To bolster up the reel-buying mood, I pulled out the old Kephart book, *Camping & Woodcraft*, and thumbed through looking for a particular passage faintly remembered. Finally I found it.

> *We would like silk tents, air mattresses, fiber packing cases, and all that sort of thing; but we would soon "go broke" if we started in at that rate. I am saying nothing about guns, rods, reels, and suchlike, because they are the things that every well conducted sportsman goes broke on anyway, as a matter of course.*

Cold mornings on the North Bank, waiting for the stove fire to start crackling and warming, I think about this paragraph of Kephart's, push my hot coffee mug up against my stomach, and consider the gorgeous photos in the fly-fishing catalogues, those fly-fishers alone in green-yellow landscapes, flylines disappearing into tree-shrouded mists. And I think about equipment, what exactly is extravagant, what is not; what is useful, what is not. I ponder just what special conduct translates to "well conducted."

Catharine asks why I clutter up the blue closet with assorted spools and lines, why one reel and one line won't do. Not being critical, she says. Just curious.

It used to be I spent almost nothing on fishing—cheap rod, cheap reel, single cracked line. But Kephart is right. Why not be "well conducted"? At least with the rod, at least with the reel, maybe skip the Gortex fishing jacket for awhile, stitch up that torn and zipperless vest, continue certain economies, but buy a couple new reels. I'm out there trading time for the experience. A good rod, a pleasant reel, a balanced line, make casting a contemplative pleasure, make the run of a good fish a musical and whistling event. Sometimes out in the crosscurrents, my arms swinging, double-hauling, I feel like Toscanini, anyway, so why not have the strings in tune?

Why not have the whole scene "well conducted"?

I looked over some reels, then, seeking the right sound. There aren't that many pawl reels that get made anymore, not well made, pawls mostly reserved for cheaper models, riveted models, everybody gone to disc brake systems. Well, not totally, thank God. I found a couple nice reels—pleasant pawl melodies in their spin, beautifully crafted, and big enough spools to hold some backing. I matched a smaller reel to my lightweight, Willie Pep rod; matched a larger reel to my middleweight, Jake Lamotta outfit; but couldn't find a pawl reel big enough for the Brown Bomber. I put one of my disc-braked reels on that. It's not, at least, a totally silent reel, has a buzzy little click incorporated that sounds like a berserk housefly. On those windy winter afternoons, gusts slugging along like a barroom drunk, I take out the heavyweight and the housefly, but somewhat reluctantly.

My trade-off for all this duffel, my economy, is to keep the Nissan one more year, rebuild the carburetor, replace the leaking sending unit, put in a new thermostat, and see if I can't nurse it along to 150,000 miles.

But the duffel feels right, feels good, feels tuned to North Bank choices. I sit at the kitchen table on rainy nights tying flies, tying leaders, patching waders, or just pulling line off the reels in long *screeeeeeeeeeeches*, finding again and again that lost chord of pawl music.

"Yikes," says Catharine, trying to read. "I'd rather you ran your fingernails down a blackboard."

Then one day we threw the bicycles on the car and headed north, biked in circles here and there, slept in odd and sundry beds, ate odd and sundry public meals, ended up coming home through Florence. I thought, why not check out this Cushner Museum thing one more time, run it to ground.

The son-in-law had reopened the place, the Cushner Fly-fishing Museum still very much alive, upstairs in a gray board house, its specialty the mounting of flies in a three-dimensional freedom.

Say they frame some photograph of a particular fly-fisher casting on a stream. Underneath, separate but yet within the frame, they suspend a few personally tied flies, flies of the fly-fisher, flies of faith. The face above, concentrating on water, has sometime, somewhere, bent over a tying vice and concentrated on these flies mounted below. This is the person, up here. This is the handiwork, below—the sense of proportion and color, the signature in fur and feather.

I looked at a series of displayed flies, many by flytiers of fame, and felt flashes in my nerve endings. These were vibrant flies, bold, defiant, glass shattering. These were flies to send me bolting home to the vice—not two golden pheasant tippets for the tail, damn it, but twenty-two! Not one body of black, but of black, and purple, and gold, each thicker than the former, mounting up thorax over thorax in a babble of sheen and flame. Not an x-long hook, but an xxx-long hook, or a tandem hook. Even the displayed nymphs and wooly-worms held the stuff of giants—double the hackle, twice the legs—revolutionary ideas. Like malaria in the blood, they will lead me on to feverish nights, Nottingham boxes piled high as a windbreak, bobbin whirling like a dervish. Certainly these flies will test my commitment to reserve and subtlety.

Curator Jack Smrekar, dark and mustachioed, told me those square-hooked old flies of mine were "sneck-hook" flies, and said to send them up. He'd forward them to Ted in Seattle, a man who went all over the country appraising collections, a man, Jack said, who would travel from Seattle to Kansas City just to check out a few flies and add to his knowledge.

A week later, under the kitchen light, I picked out thirty representative flies from the Wheatly boxes, put them in a small plastic fly box, wrapped them, and mailed them off to Jack up in Florence.

A couple months later back came news from Jack There was not much value to those flies, after all—none, in fact. Not collector's value, at any rate. I guess I might as well keep tossing them out to the pools, feeding them up one by one to whatever trout will rise.

Or I could put them back in the closet where they came from, or maybe frame ten or twelve, before the moths get them, frame them just to celebrate their subtle statement, celebrate their dark reserve, and wonder if those pigeon primary wings fluttered down from the flytier's own home loft, or if the grouse of those grouse hackles fell to his own shot in a neighboring wood.

Someone believed in these flies once, carried them sneck-hooked and lucky in the vest, and left no clear name or picture, but signed a presence with the balance of these forms.

~

Permission

A stubble-faced old Mexican told me once that, when it came to the idea of land ownership, Californians were pretty much crazy. Because, he said, the first thing they do when they buy property is put up fences, and the second thing they do is sue each other over the boundary lines.

That view maybe exaggerates a little, but to the degree it's true, it's troublesome. All across southern Oregon, over in the Bear Creek and Applegate drainages of the Rogue, for example, and over here, too, along the coast, retirees, mostly urban emigrants, have bought up considerable acreage. Their inclinations are private, their instincts defensive.

State of Jefferson secessionists, a Southern Oregon type, annually threaten to blow up Siskiyou Pass, that entry point from California into Oregon. Californians may obsess about their fence lines, but Oregon secessionists obsess about their state boundaries, and for pretty much the same reasons. Land use is not a simple issue, and the disputes take varied forms.

The Oregonian tendency to blame everything on Californians is simpleminded, without question, and blowing up Siskiyou Pass, however humorous it sounds in the abstract, in any real sense reminds me of Cuchulain fighting ocean whitecaps with his Celtic sword.

One fall a friend of a friend invited me down to some private land outside Red Bluff, California, where fishing was reputed good. We drove by jeep back through difficult lava rock country somewhere near the old Lassen Trail. I believe we unlocked with big keys something like three gates. I was told we would not be shot because the ex-green beret hired to patrol this range knew we were coming. This is the contemporary spirit manifest, and a more-or-less predictable outcome of exploding population pressures.

It's no fault of individuals, particularly, but simply the fleshing of this irony: The less one has experienced an expanse of non-threatened land in the bones of family and culture, the more one inclines to fence land, lock-gate land, post land, and patrol it with automatics.

I know a man, living up the coast a few miles, who has angered his neighbors by quietly buying up most of their water rights. He told me once about a local who drove down the private road to his place and asked to put his boat into the surf across that private land. "I told him," said my acquaintance, "this is private property."

"I understand that," said the local. "I'm asking."

"This is private property," said my acquaintance again.

"I understand that," repeated the local.

There they stood, at loggerheads, one not understanding the question, threatened by such forwardness, the other not understanding the answer, not wanting to understand it, insulted by the attitude imbedded in that answer, the inherent isolationism. More and more this happens, a new defensiveness invading the boondocks of Oregon, challenging older values of neighborliness and bounty.

I thought once to ask a newcomer over in Bear Creek drainage for permission to hunt pheasants on his acreage of cheat grass. He saw me coming on foot across his lot and unleashed two enormous dogs. They galloped towards me like the hounds of Odin. Trying my best to look nonchalant, I turned around and got back into my car. The newcomer had probably saved us both some time, but I resented his methods just a little.

I saw a sign out along the Applegate River a few years back that read like this:

No Hunting!
No Trespassing!
No Fishing!
No Hiking!
No Woodcutting!
No Nothing!

Out here along the Rogue there's a sign on the river where the Mail Boats pass, pasted up on a river-facing deck: TV BUSTED. PLEASE WAVE. But driving by that selfsame house on the up side, the road side, will net you a full compliment of NO TRESPASSING and GUARD DOG ON DUTY postings. It all sounds a little sad to me, sounds lonely and stuck, distant and buffered, like living in an isolation ward.

Recently I lived for a time in Idaho, and bought an upland hunting license, along with a fishing license. I'd drive on down from Moscow to the Clearwater River to fish for steelhead, but throw a shotgun in the back seat as another option. The Clearwater didn't have a good steelhead run that year, nobody catching much of anything, with the result that I shagged a lot of pheasants, chukars, and Huns over the breaks of the Clearwater, the Snake, and the Salmon rivers.

I discovered in southern Idaho a more frontier attitude about land. Most of the land was fenced, it was true, but not much of it was posted. I stopped at one ranch after another learning this attitude, revelling in it, marvelling at it. Before the upland season ended, landowners all over Latah, Clearwater, and Nez Percé counties had given me permission to hunt their lands, had drawn me maps, told me stories, asked to meet my wife and kids, led me out to hidden springs on their land, offered me puppies and kittens, poured me good coffee, and always supplied me with talk, good friendly talk, some of it memorable.

Several of them asked me not to hunt their land, but offered good reasons. Mostly they thought the winter had been hard on the Hun populations, numbers were down, maybe wait a year. But they poured coffee anyway, and showed me around.

I had permission-access to more land than I could possibly hunt in a season, yet kept moving on to new ranches, pulled on by the itch to see all that country, but partly, too, just wanting to meet those people, enjoy their generosity with land, almost a feeling of obligation they felt, to share it.

I met one old man out giving horseback rides to his grandchildren on a Sunday morning. He told me just where to hunt, what gates to cross, then said to come out anytime if I liked to ride. Bring the family. Use his horses. Sure, anytime.

I met one young mother who had spray painted her dog a bright orange. "Sure, you can hunt," she said. "Just don't shoot this dog for a coyote. I got him painted so you can tell."

"I don't shoot coyotes," I told her.

"Well, whatever," she said. "Either way, you can hunt."

I walked out to one farmer in a big plowed wheat field. He shut down his tractor, waited for the roar to settle out of the air, and started jawing at me. He said he didn't give permission out to hunt his land, said if he did there'd be hunters all over the place, droves of them. He asked why I wanted to go out and shoot pheasants, anyway, why I thought that was fun.

I told him that I liked to watch the dog work, and that I liked the thoughts I thought when I tromped around wheat land edges in the fall, with the colors changing and the wind sharp.

He scratched on his chin awhile, listening, spit a couple of times, let go just a trace of a smile, and said, "Sounds to me like the same reasons I go out and rod the summer-fallow. Hell, I go out there sometimes when it don't even need it. OK. You go on out there and hunt. Anytime you want."

And he started the tractor back up.

One thing for certain: nobody said to me, "This is private property," and thought that a fair and sufficient answer to the asking. Nobody's said that to me in North Bank country, either, but I'm careful about where I ask. Most of the longtime ranchers in this country, like old Johnny M., live in worn farmhouses with saddle-roofed outbuildings. I knock on those doors and find welcoming people, easy and open with their land.

During my Ashland years I sometimes winter-fished the Applegate River, a tributary of the Rogue. Winter steelhead would reach the Applegate about January, generally a decent run of them, too, but it took considerable strategy for a bank angler just to find access to the river.

Sometimes my fishing partner and I would go up to the county park above Ruch and stand elbow-to-elbow with the bait anglers, or we would go downstream and brave the Dobermans at that short unfenced stretch below the Applegate Store, or we would push through a blackberry jungle at a place we found where the river arced back from the road. Choosing this last place generally meant thorn-ripped waders. We'd reach the river, wade out to cast, and feel icy rivulets start running down our legs.

The houses along the river were mostly new and the landowners unfriendly. We asked at a number of places without any luck. One rainy Saturday afternoon we found a tractor road we had not yet explored, drove down it, and rolled over the Applegate on a bridge of cracked concrete and weathered planking. We saw no signs forbidding our presence, and no gates or fences. We parked and found a path that ran down over gravel and through bushes toward the river. Quail called from the hillside behind us. Two mallards quacked and jumped up off a back-channel slough. Everything augured well.

Then the old man appeared. He came over the bridge, and hailed us. "Afternoon," he said. He was short, straight as a fencepost, with a stern jaw. He looked like trouble.

"Afternoon."

"I own all this land." He waived upstream and downstream in a way that suggested infinite acreage.

We nodded.

"You boys catch many fish?"

"Not too many."

"Me neither," he said. "You boys find out how to catch 'em, and you let me know. That's all I ask. Just tell me where you catch 'em and how."

We fished his place off and on all that winter. We never touched a steelhead. We fell in a few times. Once we stopped at his house, a tilting brown affair, moss-covered, under a huge tree, with about two cords of hardwood piled on the porch.

"I'm a colonel," he told us. "Retired. Name's Bosworth. You boys don't seem to fish any better than I do."

We allowed as how maybe we fished worse, but it was a beautiful long stretch of river, with nice riffles and holes, and the steelhead had to be in there somewhere. We said we'd come back next winter and do better if that was all right with him. He let out a couple little barks of laughter and said that would be fine.

The following year we never fished anyplace else. My partner caught a couple of steelhead finally. Colonel Bosworth held the opinion that it might have been luck, and looked at me with commiseration.

One sunny January afternoon I drove over to the Applegate alone, stopped by the colonel's house and said hello to him, then drove on over the bridge. One of the most promising looking steelhead riffles ran just upstream of the colonel's place, his lawn running down to the tail-out, lawn chairs, picnic table, and flagpole close down to the river there, the flag always flying as it was that day.

I parked cross-river from the colonel's place and hiked upstream to the head of the riffle, waded in, laid the flyline out, held the line carefully between my fingers to feel the soft bump of a winter steelhead, if it ever came, and just then it came. I set the hook.

The fish wallowed along the surface, shook its head, and tore off downstream. I followed, playing it carefully, taking my time, figuring to keep this fish since the winter run was in no jeopardy. When the fish tired, I led it down to a gravel bar.

Just then I thought I heard music. It sounded like Sousa's "Stars and Stripes Forever." I looked across the river and saw Colonel Bosworth by the flagpole. He wore his colonel's hat. Above him the flag flapped proudly in the wind. The Sousa march, coming from the house, suspended itself over the river. The colonel looked straight at me, squared his shoulders, and saluted me—slowly, carefully, solidly, like it meant something.

I took in the gentle and funny whimsy of that stern-looking old soldier. I lifted the steelhead for him to see. Colonel Bosworth waved. I waved back.

I remember Colonel Bosworth well, and fondly. I think of him sometimes when I set out in North Bank country to find some new access point. It was like that one rainy afternoon when I tried to find the owner of some pastureland I wanted to cross. I got directed from farmhouse to farmhouse, finally found the right place with nobody home but the dogs. So I drove back down a long hill to the creek and saw a man standing out in the pasture.

"Aw, hell," he said, when I asked about access. "Nobody cares so long as you're local. Just don't mess nothin' up."

On up the creek there's a primitive camping spot, roughed-out table, shelves nailed to a myrtlewood trunk. "Use At Your Own Risk" reads the scribbled sign on the gate.

One cold morning on that creek, up above the second bridge, higher than I'd been before, my fly just swinging across a good hold and my concentration on it, I looked up and over my shoulder for no reason, and saw the man there, just behind me, his hands tucked in his bib overalls, his big shoulders swelling his shirt, a couple days' of whisker-growth on his face, tobacco-stained teeth. "Checking to see who you was," he said, a little too quietly, and waited for me to suck my heart back down to its accustomed position.

Normally I'm pretty aware of things in the woods. This guy had come up on me without cracking a twig.

I told him I was local, North Bank; told him I was a STEP volunteer; told him I generally released what few steelhead I caught, especially in this creek where the run wasn't much anymore.

He took that in, nodded a couple of time, rotated his shoulders around, and said nothing for a minute. Finally he appeared to come to some conclusion and pointed up through the trees at his house. "That's my place," he said, and proceeded on with various personal theories about why the steelhead runs were down. I didn't agree much with his theories. He said, finally, that if I wanted to, I could cut across his pastureland on the way back to my car. Just so long as I was careful with his fences.

I fish that stretch of water regularly now, and I cut across that pastureland, but I wouldn't fish there if I weren't "a local." I get the feeling that it might not be a smart thing to do.

Now it's coming on December. The Rogue is rising; all the rivers and creeks are rising. Even the seasonal creek in our back draw is starting to gurgle and hum under the cross-board plank. The yearling blacktails, out of apples, eat the fallen apple leaves. And it's getting on time for my annual visit with Rancher H. some miles to the south, make sure his gates will be unlocked to those roads through the sheep pastures, get a key if they aren't.

A couple more good rains should open up the river mouths and bring in the runs.

I can see Rancher H. pushing that black Stetson of his back from his forehead, giving me that steady, flat, considering look, saying, "I guess that would be all right," saying it in a way that makes mine a new question, and his a new answer, every single year.

And there are those places to the north, high up along the edge of North Bank country, where the river access is public, and the riverbed is public, but hiking out to the roadway at dark can pose its problems. Often as not I stumble into some place with Mary Jane growing behind the outbuildings and wormy-looking pit bulls staked in the backyards. When that happens, no matter how high up I've climbed or how dark it's getting, I always back right down again to the river and hike a good ways further. Some strange people live back in that country, some seriously paranoid people among them, I'm told. I don't even want to go up to their doors.

Permission-access is tricky business, and creates its limits. I more or less respect what limits private ownership imposes, subject maybe to some disagreements about what constitutes navigable, and therefore public, waterway. I guess that means there'll be some gaps in my mental map of this country. But the North Bank address certainly helps when talking to landowners, and working with STEP helps, and a little common courtesy goes a considerable ways. Meanwhile, the Idaho ranchers, the old Johnnys, and the Colonel Bosworths of this world hold my absolute respect and gratitude.

And I guess I'll manage to live with the rest of it.

$\sim$

For the Nose

Yearlings, long shadows, and the daytimes fill with the cider-scents of juicing. Nighttimes fill with sounds of plunking apples. The lawn is a dung heap. The animal scent of it wafts along the breezes, pleasant enough for those who like such things. The deer follow us about on the lawn expecting bread. When we climb into the apple trees to pick, the deer stand under the branches waiting for rejects. It is a worry that they will jostle our ladder. We joke about the spike-buck who frequents the side yard, how sweetly his apple-fed loins would stew, but neither Catharine nor myself feels adequate to that sort of foraging. If he trusted us less, we might consider it more.

The herons have left the rookery long since, the swallows gone from under the eaves. The rhodies lost their petals months back, about the time the smells of the wild azaleas faded. The dahlia leaves are covered with dust. Only a few blossoms remain. But the mystery weed of the Rogue gravel still crushes under my wading boots, sending up its spicy pungency. My guess: family of sage.

Yesterday I took the calico to the vet, some sort of scabby eruption on her neck. Half the cats of Gold Beach suffer this allergic affliction, it seems. No good winter freezes, said the vet; therefore, more pollens, pollens in every month, pollens in every puff of wind, dormant fleas under every leaf, and all that pollen and breeze adds to a bad environment for cats.

It adds to a bad environment for allergic humans, too. The Radio Shack in Gold Beach had a "Going out of Business" sale, largely because the owner's wife was reacting to local pollens. This the owner told me one day, wiping off empty shelves, as I fingered a last sale-item roll of speaker wire.

So far immune to allergic reactions myself, I find uses for this heavy air. It gives address to various paths and pools of the rivers.

The other day I drove up along the Rogue, fished Coal Riffle, parking above, as always, the grass dead and brown. Walking down through crisping alder leaves, pushing through the rough-skinned snake grass at the foot of the path, I could smell river moss before I'd fully crossed the clean, stone-smelling gravel bank to the river's edge. Moss proved the problem, too, my fly picking up moss on every other cast, the river turbid from rain and jetboats. But there is always this smell of stone and moss about the place, and sometimes, too, that gas-oil smell of the boat motors, a couple of private boats generally parked cross-stream. The gas-oil smell is not altogether unpleasant to me, evoking memories of Minnesota boathouses.

Nothing hit at Coal, so I drove on up toward Agnes, parked above a place I fished often, pushed down through ragweed to the familiar alder grove, on through to the boulder beach, the slick full of boats and anglers. There was scant room between them for a few casts. I smelled the Mail Boat lunches across the river while I stood there sniffing the air, and heard the shouts of the drivers, then headed back up along the path and pushed my face close to the remnant blackberries, shriveled on their vines, to smell their deep pungency.

Higher in the drainage, the water looked lower and clearer. A couple of distant fly-fishers stood waist-deep on a lower reach, so I went further upstream, walked down the familiar access road, the mountain-quail road, always a covey of them around. A new metal gate blocked the road halfway down, a NO TRESPASSING sign framed and glassed on the top of one support post. I ducked under and went on, doing no harm that I could see, taking nothing, leaving no fire rings, no beer cans, in fact piling up a few cans to carry out on the way back—a neighborly trespasser, feeling that my previous uses of this road before the new gate, before the sign, somehow gave me proprietary status, feeling, too, that the gate probably stood there to discourage those 4X4 rigs that rolled down sometimes, high-axled over the middle hump, and chewed up the riverbank. I could slide down a bank just upstream, anyway, to the public byway of riverbed, and had done it that way once or twice, except that it messed up the bank, scraped up the humus, smelling of beetles and old leaves, and filled up my waders and shirt with thorns.

It was early afternoon, the river shaded in places, as I crossed over the white-chalked boulders to the edge. An osprey came screaming down. Two chinook rolled in the pool below, big and green backed. Sounds of sawing opened up behind me, and a waft of myrtlewood scent floated in simultaneously. Somebody up there on the hillside was sawing it, filling the air with myrtlewood juices. Some people get headaches under myrtlewood trees, I'm told. For myself it is perfume, brings me back to groves on the Klamath River, dense and shiny, the ground crackling with myrtle nuts, where river days took hiatus at Ferry Point, crossing of the old Kelsey Trail, and we spread out our tarps under the myrtle groves, threw out our bags under the fragrance, and slept.

Nothing hit in the first pool, or the second, or the third, a dearth that kept me wading upstream, just edging around the deepest spots on tiptoes, myrtlewood smells fainter. Upstream above a pour-off I saw them, then, the half-pounders, first one, then others, jumping, chasing, cavorting in a wide pool, in shade of an east cliff side, a salmon rolling up there, also. I waded up above and watched them come to me, felt them bumping the nymph, not taking, and the smell of silicone grease on the new reel rose up through the river smells, rosewood handle turning smoothly, pawl music waiting to happen.

Back in Connecticut, graduate school days, along rusting trolley tracks leading out from Short Beach along the sound, I ran and reveled in smells of the salt marsh, watched upstreaming schools of bluefish and shad, and thought someone, somewhere, should make a museum of scents, olfactory culture. There's art for the eyes, music for the ears, delicacies for the palate. What for the nose?

Were I curator of such a place, my own personal nose-display would have much to do with fishing: waxed smell of a newly rubbed line, pungency of damp waders, sheepy hint in a wet wool shirt, fresh-cut ferns in a fishy wicker creel, pine needles dry in the sun. There'd be an Ely boathouse at dawn—hemp rope, wet wood where high water soaks on the log dividers, sheet metal buckets full of minnows (a few belly-up, gills pale), fresh paint, and oil that drips blue-gold on the water from the pulled up motors, kapok cushions, boat bottoms crusted with aromatic fish scales, minnow tails, dried worms, weedy-smelling minnow-tank water, the tank bottom dark with finning chubs.

There'd be the neighboring icehouse with the cold-steel smell of chisel, saw, and tongs, sweet cedar chips, dank wet sawdust on the deep-thrust shovel, fishy freshness of iced-down pike, fresh weed-smelling wind across the waves, and wafting up through all that the rubber-tire smell of the tire trough on the old hand-turned grindstone.

Down the hallway, next display, rises a sulphury Yellowstone morning, cold, mud pots boiling along boardwalks, sulphur spewing, then out the wet-wood-smelling dock to the guide boat, the inboard StarCraft, the smells of fish box, fresh grease on the battery terminals, and the cool smell of sphagnum moss in the worm can; later the blood smells of the big trout as I gutted them out to the gulls that hovered and screamed, warm and birdy, cigarette smoke from the tourists standing there, watching, faucets coppery, even the faucet water smelling of sulphur.

Further on down this nose museum hallway, around the corner, maybe I'd have the Mississaugi River, Ontario, spar varnish on the Queen's Boat, tannin-foaming water, Bert's ranger sweat, the wet-wood smell of the paddles, raw-fish sweetness of filleted pike on the back stoop, Frenchy's tarts—blueberry and mince—cooling in the back window, and the thick smell of bear, the bear cub tethered under the stoop, watching and woofing.

One cold night on the Mississaugi, we snagged our last Dare-Devil deep in a stretch of fast water. My dad sent me in after it, rope tied around my waist, rain falling, slate twilight hinting of frost, water brown and frothy, and I remember clearly standing shivering on the rocks and smelling bear-scent that blew down to us from the tumbled boulders above the falls.

It's odd, but well known, how strongly scent associations work, how the brain has its own special and primordial place for scents, the olfactory bulb. I should not be surprised, then, to find myself pleased by the gutty pungency of fishhouses, by the salty scents of old pike heads nailed to rafters. At the Gold Beach docks, at the mouth of the Rogue, where the anglers come in with their salmon and snapper, lingcod and albacore, the smells hold all the old edge for me, but basted now with barnacle and kelp. I nose up into those scents, marking them for my own.

Last week I found in the shed my opaque-white pharmacy jar of lanolin and citronella, that Horace Kephart mosquito recipe from Wisconsin days. I dusted the lid, unscrewed the cap, and ran my nose past the mouth of the jar. There rose from it again that familiar citronella smell, still strong, recalling evenings of brown trout, dapped spider-flies, stinging nettle, barbed wire. Just as I'd start back across the pine hill, my own essence of citronella would join an ether of it, blown up the path ahead of a couple old-timers, heading out for nighttime browns. I'd hear crashing and swearing along the back-path, see their bobbing flashlights, notice in their hats dry flies the size of silver dollars.

"How in the world can you guys see to fish?" I'd ask.

"Just throw it out and listen for the splat," they'd say.

That myrtle-smelling day on the North Bank stream, those half-pounders came boiling up the current from below, pushed past a rock point, into the pool. They hit the big Heron Nymph a few times, took turns leaping and throwing the hook. After losing the first two steelhead that way, I tied on a smaller fly. They hit that hard, and I got pawl music, over and over. They'd run sideways out of the pool into the shallows, then back. I horsed them in fast on the heavy leader, and they needed no pumping on the release— beautiful, fat, wild steelhead, all about twenty inches, their adipose fins high and nubby.

Of course there was that dinner date with Catharine drawing closer, a meeting for spicy burritos at El Rancho, so I hurried back downstream, bouncing through the deepest holes again on tiptoe, letting the current push me, jogging on the sand stretches, hopping fast over the shore boulders, smelling myrtlewood, a smell that would go together with the day's steelhead now, would go together with that whole school of leaping half-pounders.

The beer can pile lay at the base of the road. I shook out stale beer from the cans, stomped them, stacked them, and carried them up, then drove too fast down Jerry's Flat towards Gold Beach, without traffic to slow me, smelling the forgotten lunch banana turned brown and soft on the dashboard in the day's heat, and smelling, too, the lingering stale-beer smell of those flattened cans behind the back seat.

∼

Back to the River

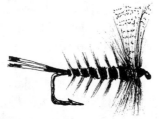

Outside of Grant's Pancake House one Sunday morning with
Catharine, after a pleasant omelet, out by our bicycles leaning on
the front flowerboxes, I heard my name spoken, looked around at
the red Corvette, and knew it was Ron Lukas, manager at the Indian
Creek Hatchery. We chatted, and he said the big smolt-release was
scheduled for the next day, the smolts prime and ready.

"We'll get started about six or so."

Ron drove off toward the Patterson Bridge. Catharine and I
bicycled inland, up past the mill and Huntley Park, over Kimball
Creek and up a steep rise, then tucked for a long coast down past
cabins and green swales, turned finally at the Lobster Creek Bridge
and stopped midway over the bridge to look down at the river. It
was up and flowing strong with a surge of dam-release water from
Lost Creek Reservoir. The water looked prime to flush smolts out
of the river system and into the sea.

So I set the alarm that night, got up early the next morning, and
drove down to Indian Creek Hatchery in morning light, six or so,
as Ron had said. Nobody there, only two Appaloosas in the pasture
rearing up against each other, nipping.

It was one of those dizzy mornings with a hint of loneliness snarled
in the myrtle leaves, and Indian Creek tumbled its way along. I
walked out toward the raceways. The smolts looked fine. The day's
doings for them would be evening doings I realized then, six or so
on the other end of the day. I looked down at the smolts' darting
energy and got a little nostalgic. A body hates to get too nostalgic
about just some fish, saying good-bye to minnows; but I felt it
anyway, all those young bodies setting forth, the way I once set
forth, the way I still sometimes set forth, but with less energy and
less ambition now, and the memory rose of the last time I'd driven
north to a river stretch I know well, and had gotten mugged, halfway

there, by another intention. The familiar water had beckoned as I'd passed it, and I'd seen my turnoff well in advance, but for some reason I'd just driven on by and kept going, setting forth on a territorial gambit, lured up farther north to a strange river I'd glimpsed once or twice, and its canyon, deep and narrow, without paths.

That drive was less than a full-blown, smolt-spirited quest, but something in the bones inspired it, some serious counterweight to home ground, some aping of the first departure.

When nobody arrived at the hatchery after fifteen minutes of smolt-watching, I knew for certain that the release would be that evening. I drove back to the North Bank place and burned off frustration with sit-ups and stretches out in the garage. Two fawns under the nearest apple tree looked curiously in through the open garage door. Smolts and fawns—the local young. I don't remember considering, when I was younger, all this stuff about home place, felt no particular need then to know the paths and the sweet spots, to feel securities of meridian. The young hold room in themselves for drifting, room for space. I don't know whether here, now, on the North Bank, with home buildings and home circlings, I simply wax less confident and flexible, or whether I misremember youth (forgetting those womb-like tree forts, for example), or whether this current narrowing of landscapes to the homey, familiar and solid, only the occasional strange canyon, soon familiar itself, shows a kind of wisdom.

That evening at the hatchery, six or so, the festivities did, in fact, begin, more hoopla than I had expected by a factor of ten—lots of faces I didn't know, men and women with regular cameras, video cameras, a NewsWatch team in a white van, Dave Harris there in blue and yellow shorts, looking happy, with a cadre of helpers in ODFW browns, our state representative present, too, and smiling, officers of Curry Anadromous Fishermen looking expansive, various volunteer feeders of the smolts, and a big white transport truck hooked up to a fire hose, getting filled with Indian Creek water.

Ron and Milt walked a seine net down the length of Raceway One. Terry, Milt, and an ODFW woman I hadn't seen before pulled on waders and crawled gently into the raceway, heedful of the plastic liner. They began scooping fish in assorted dip nets, passing them up to me and others who carried the smolts, dripping and flopping, to the truck, handed them up, waited for the empty net, and went back. Cameras flashed, newsmen on the walkway nosed big lenses down over the nets filming the flop, flop, flop of smolts, everybody pressing back and forth over the slippery cedar planking of the walkways with soaked jeans and wet shoes.

"Not too many in the nets now," called out Harris. "The weight could hurt the ones on the bottom."

Everybody grinning, laughing, festive, odd bits of dialogue filtering through the press of bodies.

"Don't drop them down there. I can't reach them under the walkway."

"What's the body weight?"

"Hand me that net there with the long handle."

Harris grinned at me and said, "I'm going back to the Umpqua. New job. Research biologist out of Roseburg. Start in September."

"Working with the Steamboaters?"

"Certainly," he said. "Remember Tom? Blonde-haired guy? He's up there now, too, doing research on cutthroat."

He moved off happily to check the raceway again. More laughter spluttered, everyone grinning, flopping fish all around my face as the nets moved by. "Arriba, arriba," I almost shouted out, remembering smelting days on the shores of Lake Michigan, people amidst plenty, dancing times.

Half the smolts got released that night, two full truckloads of smolts, seventeen thousand of the thirty-four thousand. Night release reduces predation. That's the theory.

Harris swirled his hand to signal that the truck was full enough for the first run. Workers battened the hatches and the truck rolled up the blacktop. Three ODFW people sat crowded in the front seat. Cars followed after, mine one of them, in a regular wedding procession, out past the horses, past the landing, over the Wedderburn Bridge, up the North Bank road to the Mail Boat ramp on the Rogue estuary. The truck backed down to the river as car doors slammed and the news team jogged forward with cameras in the fading light, a smell of salt and weed hanging over the dark water, and the sounds of the ocean swells breaking steadily out there to the orange-gray west.

Three extension hoses reached out to the water from the back of the truck, people under the hoses lifting them into something of a straight down-slant. A tall young ODFW man spun the worm wheel of the water valve. The hoses bucked and leaped, then spewed water and fish. "Keep it down, underwater," shouted somebody, as we all watched the bubbles and fish swooshing out, the Indian Creek water running cleaner than the Rogue and cutting a green swath through the brown, with smolts jumping along its path in surreal motion. What looked like a steelhead, or salmon jack, jumped further out, and someone said, "Must be a seal out there, chasing it."

Then we were done. All the water and fish had poured down into the Rogue with a monumental push toward beginnings. We shook out the hoses, and one last smolt dropped onto the gravel of the beach. Someone picked it up and tossed it into the river, but it was too dazed to swim, and floated, then began swimming in circles. Terry waded out and grabbed it, pumped it gently, released it again. It swam off in a straight line and everyone cheered and clapped.

Back at Indian Creek again we reloaded the truck, first with water, then with smolts, net after net of them, as before. When the truck had driven off again with its second load, heading the procession, those of us who stayed behind, to finish up, ran the seine net again, dropping screens into the raceway behind it, and started netting the last smolts over into Raceway B.

We bent our faces low to the dark water looking for the last smolt to transfer. Four of us clustered around Milt, the last netter. "There's one, there's one," we said.

Milt thought we were kidding him. "Where?" he said. "I don't see it."

Then he saw it, netted it, grinned a you-were-right grin, handed the net up, and rolled awkwardly out in those borrowed boot waders that did not fit him well.

It was over then, and the hatchery seemed suddenly quiet and unremarkable, the cars all but gone, the truck gone, most of the people gone, the evening light untangling the last of itself from the trees of the hillside.

But seventeen thousand newly planted smolts swam around down in the Rogue estuary wondering where they were, shaking dizziness from their brains, wire-code sealed in their snouts, bodies firm and healthy with fish food. Their gills would be pumping with hints of brine, their brains beginning to sense freedom, to sense the absence of raceway walls and screens. Their survival instincts would begin to hone, jumpy to shadow, prone to rock cover and branch cover, and all their senses would begin to work through time to their multiple routes past seals and gulls and egrets and herons, out over the river bar.

The following morning I drove down to visit my mother at an assisted-living place in Brookings. Unlike my father, she had survived her stroke. When I came into her room, she pointed to the cherry wood chimes-clock on her dresser. In her stumbling, approximate speech she said, "The refrigerator."

"The clock?"

"It's not dead."

She meant that the hands had stopped moving, but the clock still ticked. I said I'd take it home and fix it. A photograph of her family leaned against the clock. They stood on the shores of their own particular home river, the Mississippi, my mother a tot in pigtails, full of smile and life, Sunday hats on the older sisters, all the family facing the camera except for my grandfather. He stands sidelong to the shore, arms crossed, mustache bristling, eyes upstream on the river current, and his mind, evidently, far from the frozen-time camera, fixed instead on the flowing Mississippi.

This meddling with time, I thought, this clock that does not turn but ticks, this stop-bathed pigtailed picture of my mother that does not hold. Grandfather had it right to keep touch with the river. And the smolts have it right, too, I thought, their year of nativity imbedded in their noses, time moving in their genes, and those time-telling genes unbroken. They'll be back, undulating like pendulums, returning round their farewell jetty back to the home river. Standing there in my mother's room, broken clock in my hands, I could almost hear those smolts swimming in the spume off the Boardman coast, out beyond Cape Ferralo, fusiform chronologists of real time and sea time.

∿

A week later we did the second bunch of smolts, much the same way, but a few different faces among the volunteers, and no video-laden news crew, no state representative. We managed it some smarter, though, and lowered the raceway water periodically to make netting easier. Two more full truckloads of smolts rolled out to the estuary, and then the last load, the third load, a light one, netted out by flashlight, nothing much left to net. "There's one," we'd say.

"There's two." And we carried the ridiculously light nets up to the truck crew, to drop in one last smolt here, one last smolt there, every smolt netted out at last.

Full dark had settled, and the tank truck pulled off on its last run. I did not follow, but imagined the ODFW crew hooking up the hoses in the dark, flushing those last few smolts out into the black, waiting river.

"Time for champagne?" I asked Harris.

He patted his belly. "Maybe some skimmed milk."

"Been hooking any steelhead?" Neighbor J. asked me as we walked to our cars. "There's some coming in."

"Haven't really been out," I answered, a true enough statement, my time all spent fixing that second bathroom.

Big Charlie handed me a beer. A few of us stood around in darkness, and watched the car lights creep down over Knox's road. We lingered longer than we need have, feeling the new emptiness of the place. Everyone had a phrase of freedom, the same feeling on all our minds.

"Must feel great to those smolts to get out of those raceways."

And another, "Jesus, but it must seem like a big-assed river."

Maybe we remembered ourselves that first starless night on a prairie road, fresh out of the homestead, not much jingle in the pockets, sitting a busted suitcase in the November rain, hitching a ride to somewhere, not giving so very much of a damn just where that somewhere might be, feeling lonely and lost, but also limitless, invulnerable, and eternal—all at the same moment.

We drank our beers there in the parking lot, just the glow of a pickup cab light glimmering on our faces, then climbed into our separate cars and followed on out to Jerry's Flat Road.

Back home on the stoop I stripped off my soaked jeans and saw the mottling of white scales all over the trouser legs, smolt scales, those scales smolts drop about the time they gain their downstream urges. The scales had washed off their sides in the evening's netting and carrying, and had stuck to my pants legs like so many miniature petals. Parting remembrances, I thought them, tiny and pearly.

I brushed at them, at first, then stopped, and left the jeans on the porch, and went inside.

≈

Company

Ralph M.'s dahlia fields, up the North Bank, rows and commercial rows of them, glimmer in assorted purples, reds, oranges, whites, and yellows. They bloom over the Clay Banks of the Rogue, too high to be seen from the river. But mornings when I turn the rig at Rogue Park, drive up the North Bank toward Lobster Creek, the dahlias blaze a foreground to the river, starting the day with color. Then at night, when I drive back from fishing, there are bucks, mostly bucks, moving all along the road, once a muscled six-point stalking up from the edge of the dahlia fields out of a gray-black fog.

It is like that often: days that begin with the color of flowers, or of the turning vine maple, end in dark rides back river roads ablaze with glowing eyes, eyes of coon, possum, deer, mink, skunk, feral cat—buttons of eye-gold, night-flower correlates to the dahlia fields. Reflectors on guardrails or road markers look like animal eyes and drive my foot to the brakes. A friend told me once, "Drive that Agnes road at night and you'll see cougar."

It is deer season, rifle shots kicking across the hills, waking us sometimes in the early mornings, and I think the bucks may be bedding along the river. Or maybe they just come down at night for their water. I don't really know. But memory recalls how, in hunting seasons past, the big bucks of the inlands would come down from the timber of the hilltops and bed along the high-grass fence lines of Bear Creek Valley where my Labrador would kick them up now and again when we went out chasing pheasants, very big bucks jumping up beside us, bounding sideways, running in downhill plunges across the fields with tongues lolling wild in their panic.

Lots of coons frequent the road near Ron L.'s place just up from the dahlia fields. I know how long he's had that live trap from ODFW, how many coons he's carted up to Lobster Creek, how many neighbors' cats he's gotten by mistake. Two nights ago, coming back from a good evening at Shasta Costa Riffle, I saw three little bandits crossing the road toward his driveway. "Trouble coming," Ron would say. He'll have a hard time thinning those ranks very radically. I've tried it myself.

Worried about the old cat, with coons raiding the cat food, coons all over the stoop, I got an ODFW live trap smelling of skunk, baited it with dog food, caught two stray cats and finally a coon, a smallish coon that curled into a ball, nose under his belly in the light drizzle. I threw a tarp over him to keep him dry while I ate breakfast, then came out to find the tarp chewed to pieces. All the way up to Lobster Creek I kept checking on him in the rearview mirror, admiring his stoic silence. When I got to the bridge, and past it, and parked beside what appeared to be a pleasant stretch of coon country, I had a hard time releasing the catch of the cage door. The catch was only a wire-width away from a very active set of coon teeth.

Livetrapping coons like that, relocating them on up the river, brought with it a certain guilt. I imagined some territorial boar coon thrashing and slashing his smaller North Bank rival, driving him off, hungry, into a cold, wet, miserable landscape, no brother-company, no sister-company, no familiar hole-in-the-tree, no old calico cat to harass and rob, no local compost pit to dig up and gleefully spread about, no hollow-sounding stoop to jump on in the night.

Neighbor H. tells me there are teeth marks all around the plastic rims of his refuse cans.

"Must be coons," he says.

I allow as how he is probably right.

The other day I hauled the well-dented hard-shell kayak down out of the garage rafters, shook it around a little to discourage the black widows, threw it on the car's roof racks, and lashed it down. When the Nissan finally rolled past the last high-center hazard and down to the edge of the river I aimed at, I threw the kayak off again and strapped a rod case on the back deck of it, pulled on a wet suit, a life vest, a river helmet, and launched upstream into some of the greenest and cleanest water in the realm.

It had been a hot river, a big run of steelhead pouring into its lower pools on a rain-rise, staying there when the water dropped, for awhile at least. Now the lower pools held no steelhead, but I thought maybe in the kayak, getting up beyond the road head, I could catch up to a few laggards before they disappeared into the inaccessible canyon.

I never caught up to the main run, but a few of the rear guard cooperated, a couple at each pour-off. The paddling was fun, too, and I had already reckoned it a fine day when, weaving back down through the pudding-rock holes of that last canyon, I saw the three otter, all up on a rock together, unaware of me, grooming each other's throats. It appeared at first they were after the jugulars, but then I perceived the gentleness, the downright affection, the open-throated faith in each other, grooming that throat fur clean.

Down on the Klamath one time, just below Hamburg Falls, I walked back through some riverside snake grass, and almost stepped on an otter family, kits scurrying everywhere around under my feet, mama hissing, feinting at my legs until the kits made it to the river.

Or that eerie encounter on the Illinois some years back, a group of us boating the canyon in spring, and myself, lagging the group, dropping down through boulders and eddy-spin into a close confine of sculpted rock—I could have touched the floating otter there with my paddle blade. We looked into each other's eyes a long while, frozen with concentration.

It wasn't apprehension we shared, I don't think, but something else, some deep-felt animal connection.

The other day there were four of them, up above the Agnes Bridge, diving around in one of my favored slicks. I fished it anyway, got not even a bump, with no surprise, but harbored no hard feelings either, no more than towards the seals and sea lions of Johns Hole, all of us hunters on the same quest.

Such encounters give a lot to fishing days, critter vitality flowing out into the landscape, or critter calm ebbing down into my bones. Some nights up at Coal Riffle my casts float smoother, longer, quieter, when that herd of blacktail grazes downstream on the gravel flats. It feels like company.

The ones you don't see—they're there, too. Those big cats that nobody really sees very often, despite the stories, and the bears with their dung piles on the gravel bars, their prints in the sand—all there. Oh, sometimes I see them, the bears at least. I go a long ways back with bears.

Up on the Mississaugi, the pike river, as a kid, when I saw the biggest black I ever expect to see in my lifetime, I whistled, loud, the whole way back down the long path, carrying my string of fish, thinking that the bear might not get me, or my fish, if only I whistled.

Then that sow I never saw, but still imagine standing under, smelling her, that evening, as a kid, when I chased cubs through the dense Ontario poplars, until the ranger behind me knocked me rolling and shot. "She was on top of you," he said, sweating. But I never saw her, my eyes up on the cubs in the trees, and can only imagine now and again the black umbra above me, see the skin of her belly as she reared, and have to keep telling myself the truth of it, that I did not ever really see her.

Or that second bear in Yellowstone, the one that rose up and covered the camera lense, put its paws on my head, so I jerked my head back in through the car window, banging it on the top frame so hard my eyes spun. My father laughed so hard he couldn't drive but just sat there wiping at his eyes with the back of his hand.

Or the bear that came every night to our camp on the Gunflint, making the dog whine with fear.

Or the bear the Queen's Rangers shot and dropped not twenty yards from our tent door in the morning light.

Or that big black in the outhouse at West Thumb, some years later when I worked there, myself sick and puking in cold rain outside the door, while the bear held the dry interior, rummaging in baskets and grumbling at the stalls, until I stumbled around back and beat on the wall planking.

Or Shorty, our friend on Yellowstone Savage Row, small and cinnamon, a clown, who pranced on his hind legs for handouts.

Later still there came those grizzlies of the Donjek and the Alsek and Denali, bears with a presence. I had it in me to see them, and all that country, see it and fish it, so bought an old Jeep held together in places with duct tape and safety pins, bought a small used trailer, took the wall tent for sleeping, took the rebuilt canoe for the rivers and the lakes, and set off northerly with Catharine, two kids, and a dog.

On the Kenai a man got killed by a grizzly in the campground we'd left just the previous night. Park officials closed Sable Pass in Denali the day after we'd hiked it; somebody up there got his buttocks half ripped off by a grizzly. We hiked an old jeep road down to Dalton Post on the Klukshu River where it was said a man had lost his scalp to a grizzly the previous year. His dog brought the bear to him, scampering back for his master's help with the bear in pursuit. The man jumped in the river but didn't get his head quite far enough under the water. We walked down there to check the fishing, left the dog in the jeep, came back up the road afterward and saw the tracks where the grizzly had followed us. Up ahead we saw movement in the bushes. That spooked us to stock-still for awhile, until finally we found a piece of black plastic up there, stuck on a branch, windblown.

Stories, torn tundra, tracks, steaming mounds of dung.

Sometimes I remember these moments, old dredgings, and integrate them to new landscape, usually provoked to the process by some event, some berry-pocked dung pile on Dunkleberger Island, or a crash on the wooded bank behind Coal Riffle, the fly-fishers all stopping their casting, looking back at the hillside, looking at each other, then starting up the fishing again.

Last winter, just south of Gold Beach, a black bear bit a rancher on the leg, the rancher out walking around his barn in the dark, and the bear just reached out and bit him. It said so, at least, in the paper, the *Curry County Reporter*. The article didn't say what happened next. No wonder the Curry ranchers put bear traps in their sheep pastures.

I went up to Big Fish Riffle last week, waded out to the midriver gravel bar, fished it with the Heron Nymph. That pattern is working out well. I ran that fly through Big Fish without a touch, waded back to shore, walked back toward the tall deadhead that marks the trail, and almost put my head through an orb web, chunky spider at the center. When he felt the touch of the twig I put to him, he only twitched at first, but when I touched him again, he ran off the web, up a strand to a branch, and up the branch like a squirrel.

This morning, up past Agnes, a couple half-pounders hit my fly, but most of the run seems to have moved upriver with the last rain. I refished the morning's slick from the top with a heavy sink-tip line. Something took along the bottom, and the ripping head-tugs told me salmon. I kept this one, a bright jack, black mouthed, about six pounds.

Climbing back up the steep trail, I saw a round pinkish spider dangling on a single strand from a tree branch, just hanging there on his strand in the sun. When I touched him with a finger, pushed him a little, he ran back up his strand, taking it with him. The strand led up into shade. Only then did I think about the sun, and decide that the spider must have been sunbathing. I couldn't think what else he might have been doing just dangling there like that in sun glow on a single thread.

I like these things. I like the way downriver boats chase mergansers up past me in the evening light, the way the ospreys scream and dive. I like to find those new-hatched crawdads scooting around the shallows after a rain, and to see those bucks in headlights as I drive home, and to remember the time that buck spooked down from the Happy Camp road and jumped almost into my kayak, turning in midair like a diver, missing me by a long, black whisker.

I like to remember the frogs plopping out from the banks, *plonk*, as I walk the stones, and that time, along the Smith, driving at night through heavy rain, back from Ashland to the North Bank cabin on the last night of October, luckily no other cars on the road, when big bullfrogs came sailing out onto the blacktop from both sides, legs suspended like landing gear, eyes gleaming in rain-pour. There must have been fifty frogs like that in five miles along the North Bank Smith cutoff—lightning, thunder, and frogs. Something about the rain and the season got them going, traveling, checking out new spots, looking for new mud holes.

It slowed me way down. They kept jumping out unexpectedly, and I'd swerve and dodge to miss them. They were all very intently going somewhere, and I wanted them to get there. That seemed only right. We were all going somewhere. And I think I did miss them all, though in the black hurdy-gurdy and puddle-splash of the storm, it was hard to be certain.

~

Berries and Horses

A big December storm hit in the night. Rain beat down, swatting at the cabin in the gusting wind. Thunder grumbled up the valley. The hanging geranium on the stoop spun and spun. The too-heavy wind chimes finally clanged. The big pines on the south side screamed as they tossed. Pieces of pine, cones and branches, hurtled into the windows and against the sides of the cabin, banging, clattering. Catharine and I lay in bed on our backs, looked up out the window at the tall pines, three of them within our view, backlit by a veiled moon. The branches of the pines kept popping and cracking like whips.

All that energy came down through the windows and the roof, and, by some ancient and mysterious method, moved around in the bedroom like a gibbering ghost. I could not sleep, but watched and listened, having thirsted some time for such a storm, only teased, those many Ashland years, by dry lightning shows over the shoulders of Grizzly Mountain. I have missed real thunder and blow the way I have missed those massive midwestern cottonwoods, their leaves like oboes in the yellow-skied storm winds of summer.

In the morning the Rogue was backed up almost over Johns Island. The Snag Patch channel ran nearly as wide as the Rogue itself. An unusually high tide contributed to the backup, and, we knew from experience, would make for a frothy coastline. Somewhere deep in the closest holly tree the Anna's hummingbird had clutched its way to survival and darted out to the feeder for a morning sip of sugar water, as though nothing much had happened in its life, then buzzed back again to its usual holly-tree perch.

The two yearling blacktails were out, as well, looking dry and toasty in their winter coats, browsing on our ornamentals. I went out on the stoop and shouted at them. "Off you go!" They trotted towards me, instead, expecting handouts, fuzzy black-lined ears perked high, fawn-small noses snuffing.

The yard was littered with broken pine branches the size of baseball bats, and tip-sprigs enough for a few dozen wreaths. Two medium-large pines had toppled on the back ridge. We hiked up to inspect the damage, saw that the bases had snapped off above the root wads and were oozing fresh pine juices. We noticed, too, that both our fallen pines aligned perfectly with an open wind-lane left by the felling, some months back, of a south pine on a neighbor's property.

But the cabin was intact, no shingles missing, only a few dozen dangling pine boughs to clean out of the gutters.

I have almost finished the cabin interior. Only that last blue door remains to strip and stain. Last week I put in one of those motion-activated security lights over the stoop. This facilitates the lives of cats and coons in the night, and lets Catharine, arriving home in darkness, find the door lock with her key. There are more hanging geraniums and lobelias under the eaves than formerly, signs of home ground, and I am starting to hear murmurs about more dahlia beds, a deer fence, and a vegetable garden.

I spent the morning cleaning the branches out of the yard and off the roof, piling them up for a bonfire some dry day, occasionally sniffing the jaunty December camellias, and got just wet enough, and dirty enough, to move on to those blackberries encroaching along the cabin's south side and down along the access driveway. The blackberry tendrils reached out and grabbed at my arms. I cut them back but not too radically. I have nothing against blackberry pie come next fall, or a few sweet thimbles on the oatmeal.

Yard chores finished, I figured it must be getting about time to check Euchre Creek for salmon, though it was too cold and wet to take the bicycle, cloud banks still hanging to the south, snow on the cross-river hills, a touch of drizzle. I took the car.

Driving up 101 past Nesika Beach with big surf rolling, I got about even with the rest stop area and the sun broke through in a big daystar smile on the near surf, turned it blindingly white, green surf behind, Sister Rocks dark behind mist, Humbug Mountain hung with its own purple weather, beach grass glowing yellow.

I parked down at the '27 bridge, took off my white baseball hat, put on the Polaroids, peered over the bridge railing, and looked downstream, checking the south bank hole, then crossed the road, peered over the other side, the better spot. Nothing held in either place, no undulating form of chinook.

While I stood there, I checked out the adjacent fields, no cattle, no sheep, one egret up by a distant meadow puddle. The apple trees out to the south still had all their branches, it looked like, leaning braces still holding. The smooth green-brown creek water flowed down from between those upstream willows. Everything looked right and ready, just waiting to see what runs would come. The creek mouth most probably would have busted through the blocking beach sand with this last surge of water, would lie open to whatever nosing chinook decided to try it, but creek mouths are tricky. I thought maybe I should go down there and check the creek mouth. Or maybe I should first phone John Wilson to see if he had checked it.

If I see salmon anytime up here, I am supposed to call Tim at ODFW, who will get a crew out to seine. That's the program for the year, an intent to get some indigenous brood stock instead of Elk River stock, an intent to catch what we can, put them into perforated PVC piping to keep them from thrashing, and haul them up to Elk Creek Hatchery for holding until they come ripe. Then to the stripping boards with them, where blood, eggs, and milt all mingle— death and conception fish-slimed together in a hatchery-deck mating.

The Curry Anadromous Fishermen's meeting last Wednesday night featured stream reports. Steelhead counts are down, Gold Ray Dam count at a ten-year low. But ODFW divers found salmon in all the major feeder creeks of the lower Rogue—Lobster, Quosatana, Jim Hunt, Indian—in good numbers, and salmon counts looked good in the main Rogue, both chinook and coho, lots of brood stock already seined for Indian Creek Hatchery, over eighty thousand eggs stripped, double last year's number, the eggs all in their dark trays, perking in the holding room—fertilized, rosy, and round.

Feelings of optimism filled the meeting's smoky air, smiles and bonhomie, feelings of good work coming, and good work past, maybe those previous low counts just part of the cycle, or maybe the hatchery efforts paying dividends. Maybe both.

I drove home in darkness, wondering, a feral cat slinking away into roadside bushes, eye-buttons blinking out. Halfway home, I put hatchery matters behind me and thought where next I should circle, where next I should explore, what next river canyon waited.

Two days later I drove north, parked along a river access road, pulled on the waders, threaded up the rod, and walked a slant down into cedars. When I cut back and down a steep clay bank, my feet started slipping under crosswise fallen logs. It was difficult going. I cut north along a cliff edge and found an old camp fire pit in the midst of myrtle. From there I peered down at the river far below, and realized I was going the wrong way. The place I remembered from a summertime wade lay to the south.

Reversing direction brought me to a series of deep creek beds, one I wasn't sure I could escape after dropping down into it, high crumbling clay banks flanking both sides. Finally a game path crossed it, and I followed that up and out, but found myself three-sided within thickets of blackberry and blue-stalked salmonberry. I paused and thought about those blackberries.

A few years back an old gentleman over in Ashland went out for a walk by Emigrant Lake, somehow fell over into a blackberry patch, and the more he floundered around trying to get up, the more the patch grabbed him, tendrils around his arms and legs, thorns holding his clothing. He lay there for almost two days, face up. I expect he grew tired of watching the clouds scud by overhead, and the stars circle. Searchers found him there, and said if they hadn't found him, he'd have dried up like a raisin.

Buried or "berried," it's pretty much the same idea. Get stuck in those thorny stalks, wrapped up like a fly in a tendril web, and there's no going much of anywhere. The blackberry is like that, and suggests to me past ways, past places, past dreams that pluck and tear at the sleeve. There are mind-thickets to push through in this process of changing ground, and places to carefully circle.

Facing blackberry thickets, then, as I explored that unfamiliar canyon, I went around them, through the salmonberries, and finally reached a myrtlewood glade. The glade held no underbrush at all, just the high glittering leaves overhead, and the thick trunks of the trees. The ground was strewn with myrtle nuts that popped and crackled under my feet.

I rested there, rubbing at some stickers in my hands, then cut up a game trail through low brush, down another long clay bank to a park-like flatland. Elk droppings lay everywhere, the grass short, thick, and intensely green. Blackberry vines had grown high into all the low alders, their tendrils sweeping back down again like the branches of weeping willow.

From there the opposite gravel bank of the river showed itself, not far below me. The churning sounds of current rose up. Only one last barrier of blackberries separated me then from riverbank gravel, but the barrier held thick with dead stalks and caught leaves. I pushed into it a ways and saw under the thicket a deep feeder-creek channel, impossible to cross.

Thorns stuck to me, teasing and pulling, as I backed away. A half mile upriver the feeder-creek channel finally shallowed, the blackberries thinned, and a game trail crossed through to the river.

I crossed onto a grassy plateau lined for as far as I could see downstream with blackberry clumps and a jagged back row of tendrils. The blackberry leaves were wintergreen under the bare reaching alders. From there, a slide down a gravel bank and a short walk brought me to the river slick I remembered, looking more perfect than I had dared hope. Crows cawed at me from a downstream snag.

The river bent slightly around a large protruding rock face on the far side, dropped in a riffling glide as it turned, then slowed into a far pocket of holding water. I fished the nearer water without a touch. Lengthening the casts still brought nothing. I waded out as deep as I dared and aimed for the farthest pocket of holding-water. It was a long cast, five loops of running line in my mouth, one in my hand. The cast crooked a little upstream on the drop, floated a moment, then stopped. The fish shook its head and ran.

I pulled her in close at last, a bright female, about six pounds, unhooked and released her, and checked my watch—four thirty, an hour to darkness. I stood in shallows and thought about those hillside blackberries and feeder-creek channel blackberries. I imagined fighting my way back through them to the road. I didn't want to do that in the dark, but I didn't want to stop fishing, either.

I waded again into the river, rushing the fishing with worry, thinking to drift just a few more casts through that far pocket, just to see. When I cast, again the line stopped in its drift, and another fish ran.

The two were almost identical in the place they held, the way they took the fly, the way they charged downstream. The second steelhead, also a female, was larger, about eight pounds. Her first rush pulled my feet off their tentative hold, pulled me bouncing downstream, water at the lip of the wader tops. I landed her downstream, released her, and remembered, with a sweet sweep of feeling, how one time I had caught a double like this against a far rock face on the North Umpqua. Two long casts, two bright fish.

Something touched me about the mirrored image, about the merged and almost simultaneous foreness and afterness of the moment. I liked the feeling of replication, the feeling of the river merging with my idea of home water into a kind of miraculous space. I had not thought I would catch a double again in such a perfect way. It raised an odd, almost primitive excitement in me.

The sun dropped behind the west ridge. The day seemed full, but maybe more to come, unless there were an easier way back. Tall pines poked up to the east, upstream, and I walked toward them along the grassy plateau until I came close, blocked again by blackberries. But a small pathway cut under the berries. I got down and crawled along the path, through a low arch, lost my hat, stuck in thorns, reached back and yanked it free, crawled on, bellying, until I was through them. Then up a steep bank, through pine woods to a hill, up that hill to a field, on through the field. And there was the road. Once past those blackberries, it was easy going.

A few months ago, upstream of the Agnes Bridge, I watched a hawk dive into a blackberry thicket after a mountain quail, and disappear amid an impressive rattling of pinions, yellow talons overwhelmed by a thousand green talons of thorn. The hawk finally emerged in a flapping hop at the thicket's base, thoroughly disgusted, it appeared to me, thoroughly "berried," and had flown to a nearby pine to tend its disordered feathers.

Maybe, without identical steelhead, I might have felt like that hawk, felt tattered, beaten, escaping back to the road with thorns in my hat. Maybe, too, without the knowing, now, this new sweet spot of water, I might have felt disappointment, felt thorned and berried by the vaporous riverscapes of this new country.

But I felt none of that, not now with the water there reinventing itself in a familiar drift, not now with a new path down, and a new memory at its end.

I felt not berried at all, no clabbering, and walked up the road in growing darkness, feeling, if anything, the blackberry pluck of old times, old landscapes, pulling to different shapes, different contours, but not so very distant from where I had begun. I sensed a puzzle-piece fit to a space, giving that space meaning, texture, connection—

multum in parvo, chalky green water under a rock face, like someplace I had fished before. I felt old feelings, familiar footings.

Something moved forward in me, marched beside me, keeping time with my crunching footsteps on the road.

Back at the car there were horses grazing along the roadside. They watched as I put away the fly rod and pulled off my waders. They watched as I pulled a bagel and a bottle of water from a lunch sack. A big block-headed sorrel started my way, then a palomino. I climbed into the car and rolled down the window. Two soft noses pushed through, big eyelashes batting at me. I rolled the window back up and ate my bagel.

More horses came over. They kept circling the car pushing their noses up against the windows like inquisitive children. I felt welcomed. I felt at home. This was a landscape, I realized, that had grown, as that odd phrase puts it, "strangely familiar." It was gathered, mapped, ribboned, riffled, and confluenced. Most of the paths and roads were familiar. Most of the riverbanks and canyons were familiar. And except for that blue door, I'd pretty much finished the North Bank place to the contours of recollection.

Now there were these horses—sorrel, dun, palomino. I liked them in this scene. I wanted them to stay a part of it, solidly there under the oaks. They felt inland and homey to me, familiar figures in those middle landscapes of my recollection. Next time up here, I thought, I'd better bring along a few extra bagels for them, friendship offerings, and maybe a couple of apples. I wanted their eyelashes batting at my car windows. I wanted their graceful bodies pushing and circling around me. I wanted their happy, horsey smells hanging in the December air.

~